Developing **Portfolios**
for **Authentic**
Assessment,
PreK–3

Guiding Potential in Young Learners

Developing **Portfolios** for **Authentic Assessment,**
PreK–3

Guiding Potential in Young Learners

Bertie Kingore

CORWIN PRESS
A SAGE Company
Thousand Oaks, CA 91320

For information:

Corwin Press, Inc.
A SAGE Company
2455 Teller Road
Thousand Oaks, California 91320
E-mail: order@corwinpress.com

SAGE Ltd.
6 Bonhill Street
London EC2A 4PU
United Kingdom

SAGE India Pvt. Ltd.
M-32 Market
Greater Kailash I
New Delhi 110 048 India

SAGE Asia-Pacific Pte. Ltd.
33 Pekin Street #02-01
Far East Square
Singapore 048763

Printed in the United States of America

Library of Congress Cataloging-in-Publication Data

Kingore, Bertie W.
Developing portfolios for authentic assessment, PreK-3 : guiding
potential in young learners / Bertie Kingore.
    p. cm.
Includes bibliographical references and index.
ISBN 978-1-4129-5482-2 (cloth)
ISBN 978-1-4129-5483-9 (pbk.)
  1. Portfolios in education—United States. I. Title.

LB1029.P67K552 2008
372.126—dc22

2007040314

This book is printed on acid-free paper.

07 08 09 10 11 10 9 8 7 6 5 4 3 2 1

Acquisitions Editor:	Stacy Wagner
Managing Editor:	Jessica Allan
Editorial Assistant:	Joanna Coelho
Production Editor:	Appingo Publishing Services
Cover Designer:	Lisa Riley
Graphic Designer:	Lisa Miller

Contents

Acknowledgments

Corwin Press wishes to thank the following peer reviewers for their editorial insight and guidance:

Margaret Aghili, NBCT
Second-Grade Teacher
Monte Vista Elementary School
Los Angeles Unified School District
Los Angeles, CA

Amy Augenblick
Executive Director
Foundations for Families
Alexandria, VA

Susan Belgrad
Associate Professor of Elementary Education
Michael D. Eisner College of Education
California State University
Northridge, CA

Diana L. Haleman
Associate Professor
Morehead State University
Morehead, KY

Susan N. Imamura
Principal
Manoa Elementary School
Honolulu, HI

Sue Javid
Early Childhood Consultant
SCJ Associates, LLC
Bloomfield Hills, MI

Katina Keener
Second-Grade Teacher
T. C. Walker Elementary
Gloucester, VA

Marianne Lucas Lescher
Principal
Kyrene de la Mariposa Elementary School
Tempe, AZ

Shannan McNair
Associate Professor of Education
Oakland University
Rochester, MI

Miranda Moe
Kindergarten Teacher/New Teacher Facilitator
Beaver Dam Unified School District
Beaver Dam, WI

Rachel Weaver Rivera
Art Education Consultant
Imagine Art Studio
Hinsdale, IL

Cynthia Woods, 2004 NBCT
2004 Presidential Awardee in Mathematics
Wayne County Schools
Monticello, KY

About the Author

 **Bertie Kingore** is an international consultant and the author of twenty-three books, numerous articles, and instructional aids. She has received many honors including the Legacy Award as the author of the 2005 Educator Book of the Year and the Outstanding Alumnus Award from the University of North Texas where she earned her PhD. She was also the first recipient of the Texas Gifted Educator of the Year Award.

Dr. Kingore works with teachers and models instruction in classrooms all over the globe. She is recognized for her child-centered approach and her ability to weave research into practice seamlessly. She advocates learning experiences that respond to the marvelous diversity of children, encourage high-level responses and high achievement, and minimize the intensity of teacher preparation time.

She fell in love with children and the values of portfolios her first year of teaching more than thirty years ago. She delights in helping other teachers make authentic assessment realistic.

1

Assessing Young Children

Seven Blind Mice by Ed Young (1992) retells the classic poem by John Godfrey Saxe. In Young's award-winning version, seven blind mice each investigate an elephant from a narrow point of view. It is only when their perspectives are combined that a view of the whole elephant emerges. The insightful moral of this book is "Knowing in part may make a fine tale, but wisdom comes from seeing the whole." To expand upon that moral, I propose an assessment analogy. "Standardized tests and grades make a fine tale, but understanding comes from viewing the whole child and that goal is best accomplished through portfolios and other authentic assessments."

Authentic assessment is more similar to a videotape than a photograph; it is a view over time rather than a moment-in-time snapshot. Young children reveal their capacities and potentials in subtle ways that early childhood teachers access through nuanced observations and interpretations. It is paramount to collect multiple facets of data to guide understanding and decision making regarding the many aspects of children's readiness and modes of learning (National Association for the Education of Young Children & National Association of Early Childhood Specialists in State Departments of Education [NAEYC & NAECS/SDE], 2003).

While standardized testing remains a staple in American education systems, early childhood teachers seek ways to balance that data with authentic assessment procedures reflecting the whole child—emotionally, socially, and physically as well as academically (Commission on the Whole Child, 2007; Noddings, 2005). Assessment should provide a more complete picture of the developing child and be concerned about more than the measurable. As Eisner (2005) elaborated, "Not everything that matters is measurable, and not everything that is measurable matters" (p. 16). Compared to traditional assessment techniques such as paper-and-pencil tests authentic assessment techniques provide a more comprehensive picture of what the learner knows, understands, and is able to do (Erickson, 2007). The No Child Left Behind Act, while mostly associated with state academic assessments to determine adequate yearly progress, also advocates assessment based on systematic observations by teachers of children performing academic tasks that are part of their daily classroom experience.

Assessment needs to be a natural, continual component in early childhood classrooms. It is integral to teaching and learning and is a major factor guiding instructional decisions of how and what is taught and how and what children learn. Scott-Little, Kagan, and Frelow (2003) explained the relationship among standards, curriculum, and assessment by noting that standards articulate what children should learn, curriculum dictates how children will learn the required standards, and assessments measure how effectively the standards and curriculum are implemented.

This chapter presents the goals of authentic assessment and discusses the use of portfolios to attain those goals. A chart of assessment methods explains multiple appropriate assessment techniques and potential applications to facilitate teachers' decisions regarding which techniques to combine with portfolios into effective assessment systems in prekindergarten through third-grade classrooms. The chapter concludes with a brief review of the research related to early childhood portfolios and assessment as well as a list of key assessment terms and explanations as a succinct reference point to clarify applications.

AUTHENTIC ASSESSMENT GOALS

As Shepard, Kagan, and Wirtz (1998) stated, the major purpose of early childhood assessment is to guide and improve instructional practice while providing a means of understanding how young children are developing competencies. Teachers assess what is happening in the classroom and how to change things to better support children's learning. Therefore, the assessment of young children should center on classroom-based evidence of learning tied to experiences in which children play, engage in conversations, and construct meaning (Jones, 2003). Effective assessment practices dictate that the use of individually administered, norm-referenced tests should be limited (NAEYC & NAECS/SDE, 2003) and that the determination of assessment methods and strategies should evolve from the following goals:

1. Assessment supports the objectives of curriculum and instruction, measures what is educationally significant, and furnishes useful information to teachers and children.

2. Assessment incorporates multiple tools and procedures appropriate to the characteristics of the individual and the group population, including

age, language, ethnicity, economic status, and prior opportunities to experience academic learning (Association for Supervision and Curriculum Development [ASCD], 2006a; Payne, 2003).

3. Assessment tools and procedures acknowledge individual variations in learners, are responsive to children with learning differences, and accommodate diverse styles and rates of learning.

4. Assessment evidence is gathered over time from situations reflecting children's actual performance and daily activities.

5. Assessment data provides concrete evidence of progress to share with families and other invested adults.

6. Assessment information must be used to benefit children, improve learning by adapting curriculum and instruction, communicate with families, and improve the program by evaluating program effectiveness (Commission on the Whole Child, 2007; National Association for the Education of Young Children [NAEYC], 1997).

WHAT IS THE VALUE OF A PORTFOLIO?

Portfolios directly respond to the previously mentioned assessment goals. Portfolios are tools that provide educators and children with an excellent means of collecting varied evidence of children's learning achievements and assembling that documentation into a coherent whole (Stiggins, 2005). Numerous assessment experts and national organizations recommend portfolios as a key component in an authentic assessment system because of their multiple applications (ASCD, 2006a; Burke, 2005; Herman, Baker, & Linn, 2004; MacDonald, 2005; NAEYC & NAECS/SDE, 2003; National Council of Teachers of Mathematics & National Association for the Education of Young Children [NCTM & NAEYC], 2002; Stiggins, 2005). Portfolios can be used as

- feedback to students for enhanced self-concept and goal setting as children view how they have changed as learners over time;
- opportunities for children to self-assess and reflect upon their work;
- demonstrations of children's effort, preferred modes of learning, transfer of skills, and conceptual understanding;
- communication tools among children, families, and educators;
- documentation of conference information using concrete examples to illustrate achievement and instructional assessments to parents;
- connections between prior knowledge and current learning;
- support for and substantiation of special learning accommodations;
- feedback to teachers as they monitor and improve instruction in the classroom.

Consistent with developmentally appropriate practices, portfolios encourage the capabilities of all children regardless of their current levels of development. After two or three months, children can view the earlier work in their portfolios and see growth. If they are working at grade level, below grade level, or beyond grade level, the portfolio validates that they are learning and making progress.

"Assessing young children is an art; early childhood teachers are the artists applying a wide palate of techniques to paint a clear portrait of children's learning."

In classrooms, teachers' assessment practices incorporate multiple methods involving observation, inferences, and data measurements to determine what children know, understand, and can do. Multiple measures mean better accountability and better data to help each child succeed (ASCD, 2006a; Jones, 2003; NAEYC & NAECS/SDE, 2003; NCTM & NAEYC, 2002). Descriptions of a variety of techniques and of how to use each (Figure 1.1) provide a menu of options to assess children's learning.

To create an assessment system, teachers and administrators determine which combination of tools is the most effective and efficient means of collecting and recording the desired data. The system must efficiently balance the time and effort expended by students and teachers with the quality and usefulness of the procured information (NAEYC & NAECS/SDE, 2003). As teachers become comfortable with certain kinds of assessments, they can incorporate additional or different methods to ensure a more complete view of children's capabilities and progress.

Determining or adapting methods of assessment is a collaborative process between teachers and administrators because an assessment system cannot survive without administrative guidance and support (Jones, 2003). The system also requires an informed person or group within the school with a deep knowledge of how young children learn and how to align assessments to learning goals.

Regardless of which assessment methods teachers select, teachers need time to review and reflect upon the collected information. For authentic assessment to be successful, Ratcliff (2001) cautioned that teachers must take time to think about what children demonstrate and what skills need to be further developed. Regularly scheduling this time enables teachers to develop understandings of children's progress and respond to that understanding by planning appropriate continuous learning experiences.

Figure 1.1

Methods of Assessment

ASSESSMENT METHOD	EXPLANATION This assessment tool is	PURPOSE This assessment tool is used to
Anecdotal record	An informal record of an observed event or behavior.	Document a teacher's insights and observations about children's capabilities and needs during classroom activities.
Audiotape recording	A recording of a child's oral reading, retelling, or dictation in response to an authentic learning task.	Assess vocabulary, processes and achievement levels in an authentic learning situation. Document the tape's content by summarizing assessment conclusions on a rubric, check-list, or anecdotal record.
Checklist	A list of standards, skills, or behaviors applicable to learning and achievement.	Guide and succinctly record observations of standards and skills applications.
Conference–informal or formal	An informal or formal achieve-ment conversation involving teacher, child, peer, and/or family members.	Facilitate one-on-one feedback and information exchanges; elicit a child's vocabulary and perception of achievement; review and set goals.
Demonstration	An assessment of a student performing authentic tasks associated with standards.	Assess processes and product in an authentic learning situation.
Discussion	An informal, interactive, and inquiry-based conversation among teachers and children.	Assess vocabulary, content integration, and a student's perception of the content or concepts; document with a rubric, checklist, or anecdotal record.
Graphic organizer	A spatial device assessing the relationships among content and concepts.	Assess concept complexity, depth, and relationships.
Interest inventory or interview	An informal assessment of a child's interests and experiences.	Provide information about experiences and preferences to customize a student's learning opportunities.
Journals	A running record by children of their responses to learning experiences, particularly in math, science, and language arts.	Assess children's communication skills, concept applications, and reflections of their capabilities and attitudes.

Methods of Assessment

ASSESSMENT METHOD	EXPLANATION This assessment tool is	PURPOSE This assessment tool is used to
Learning log	A record of skills, learning responses, and reflections over time.	Provide information about a student's perceptions, acquisition of skills, development, and learning changes over a period of time.
Math problem solving	A demonstration of a child's application of concepts and skills in math.	Provide an authentic measure of a student's problem solving skills and understanding of mathematical concepts; recognize original thinking.
Observation	A teacher formally or informally watches children and records information during a classroom learning experience.	Analyze productive or nonproductive learning behaviors and the application of skills.
Performance or performance task	A demonstration of a child performing authentic learning tasks associated with standards.	Analyze applications of several skills, processes, and products in an authentic learning experience.
Portfolio	A child's collection over time of products that are examples of significant and representative learning achievements.	Analyze complexity, depth, achievement, and growth over time; clarify students' strengths and modalities.
Project or cooperative task	A learning task associated with standards; completed by a student or small group.	Assess content integration through product, process, communication, and cooperative group efforts.
Questioning or inquiry	An informal, interactive, inquiry-based assessment that is usually oral.	Assess content integration and a student's perception of achievement; document with a rubric, checklist, or anecdotal record.
Reading sample or running record	A record of independent reading of fiction and nonfiction to assess the level and pace of a child's literacy development.	Identify a child's reading levels, use of reading strategies, and implications for instruction.
Retelling	A learning task requiring a child to retell a story or process–usually oral.	Identify a student's vocabulary, content comprehension, sequence and organization, use of reading strategies, and implications for instruction.

Methods of Assessment

ASSESSMENT METHOD	EXPLANATION This assessment tool is	PURPOSE This assessment tool is used to
Retelling	A learning task requiring a child to retell a story or process–usually oral.	Identify a student's vocabulary, content comprehension, sequence and organization, use of reading strategies, and implications for instruction.
Rubric	An evaluative device specifying criteria and levels of quality for a learning task.	Provide a standard of quality for achievement and grading; provide a quality target for students.
Self-assessment	An assessment format used by children to assess their level of skills, learning behaviors, and achievement.	Help a student recognize levels of expectations and standards of quality; encourage goal setting.
Standardized test	A commercial, formal, norm-referenced or criterion-referenced test of specific content.	Allow for districtwide or nationwide comparisons of achievement.
Unit test–teacher developed	A teacher-prepared test for a segment of instruction.	Diagnose and compare summary information regarding achievement of learning goals.
Written work	An assessment of a child's application of concepts and skills in written work.	Provide an authentic measure of a student's composition skill and acquisition of content-related concepts and skills.

RESEARCH RELATED TO PORTFOLIOS AND ASSESSMENT

Assessment must be evidence-based and multifaceted to accurately document young children's learning (National Association of Elementary School Principals & Collaborative Communications Group [NAESP & CCG], 2005; NAEYC & NAECS/SDE, 2003). It must incorporate multiple modalities, high-level thinking, and active engagement and support authentic, high-quality learning experiences. Assessment decisions evolve from a research base regarding effective early childhood education. Research testifies to the importance of quality programs, evidenced-based instructional strategies, vocabulary development, parental involvement, teacher effectiveness, and student reflection.

Quality

The High/Scope Educational Research Foundation's (2005) longitudinal study and Karoly's (2005) report make it apparent that high-quality early childhood programs significantly affect children's life success. Children from poverty and young children with special needs experience higher academic success and fewer social-emotional problems when they participate in a quality-based program

(Nelson, 2006). Rothstein (2006) asserted that the quality of the program is as important as the existence of such programs themselves.

We know curricula and instruction that engage children as active learners; efficient and effective administration that focuses on the needs and desires of children, families, and staff (NAESP 2005); and ample time and teacher support for children to be involved in play to explore and manipulate materials, concepts, and ideas (MacDonald, 2005; NCTM & NAEYC, 2002) characterize high-quality early childhood programs (High/Scope Educational Research Foundation, 2005; Marcon, 2002). Drawing upon the work of Vygotsky (1962), teachers instruct at levels that are challenging but attainable. Since students' zone of proximal development varies, children experience demonstrations of instruction at different levels (Berk & Winsler, 1995). Assessment methods should be tied to children's daily activities that support children's learning, elicit their perspectives on learning, and teach standards of quality (NAEYC & NAECS/SDE, 2003; Potter, 1999).

High-level thinking continues to play a vital role in learning and long-term achievement for all children (Anderson & Krathwohl, 2001). Ensure that students' thinking progresses from the beginning levels toward more complex levels because knowledge and skills are necessary but not sufficient elements of understanding for long-term retention and achievement (Shepard, 1997; Wiggins & McTighe, 2005; Willis, 2006). Assessment methods should reflect high-level thinking opportunities more than simple, correct answers.

Portfolios and assessment work in tandem with solid instruction to guide and enhance children's potential. Connecting learning experiences appear in several chapters to connect the assessment or evaluation procedure that is being discussed to a classroom learning experience. A template is repeatedly used to frame these examples and signal the reader.

Research-Based Instructional Strategies

Strategies proven through research to have the highest effect on achievement should guide decisions regarding which strategies to apply most frequently in instruction and assessment. Strategies with the highest potential for achievement gains such as similarities-differences and summarization become priorities in instruction (Marzano, Pickering, & Pollock, 2001). Since similarities-differences involve categorization, comparison, and analogous thinking, early childhood learning experiences and assessments incorporate those high-yield strategies frequently. To engage young children in similarities-differences, teachers plan experiences and assessment requiring sorting and grouping, compare and contrast, and oral analogies, such as "A child talking is like a bird _____," and "How is a watch like a calendar?"

Understanding increases when the brain seeks meaning by connecting the unknown to what is known and when there is an emotional response integrated into a learning experience (Caine, Caine, Klimek, & McClintic, 2004; Sousa, 2001; Sylwester, 2003). Thus teachers engage children in learning experiences and assessments that build upon prior experiences, interests, sensory explorations, and emotional engagement. A nonthreatening environment is maintained during instruction and assessment to allow children to succeed. The goal is an appropriate balance between just enough versus too much challenge (NAEYC, 1997).

Effective instruction responds to multiple modes of learning and how students learn best (Gardner, 1996; Grigorenko & Sternberg, 1997; Willis, 2006). Teachers incorporate multiple learning pathways because the more ways information is introduced to the brain the more dendritic pathways of access are created to enhance memory (Willis, 2006). Teachers plan instruction and assessment to activate both mental engagement and process engagement because students' active involvement and personal processing of information increase their understanding and retention.

Vocabulary

Recent research clarifies the synergistic relationship of comprehension and vocabulary (Marzano, 2004; National Reading Panel [NRP], 2000). Specifically, vocabulary is directly related to comprehension and learning achievement. Children's vocabulary level at the beginning of first grade predicts their reading ability at the end of first grade as well as their eleventh-grade reading comprehension (Marzano, 2004). Sustained silent reading and direct instruction in subject-specific vocabulary emerge as the two approaches that combine to help rescue low achievers and enhance the academic achievement of all students (ASCD, 2006b). Frequently read aloud to children and provide ample opportunities for them to individually explore both fiction and nonfiction. Consistently use specific words in context such as *alphabet* rather than *ABCs* and *equation* rather than *number sentence,* so young children have the benefit of enriched vocabularies that increase their achievement potential. Conversations with children, inquiry, tape recordings, and child-involved conferences are examples of assessments that document vocabulary development.

Parents and Families

Research documents that a substantial outreach to parents positively affects young children's learning and long-term achievement (High/Scope Educational Research Foundation, 2005). Furthermore, one aspect of the No Child Left Behind Act is to promote informed parents through an education system that is transparent and responsive to the needs of parents and children (Spellings, 2007). Family members and educators benefit from a collaborative attitude of mutual respect, cooperation, and shared responsibility as they engage in an ongoing information exchange about a child (Commission on the Whole Child, 2007; NAESP & CCG, 2005; NAEYC & NAECS/SDE, 2003).

Parents are both a valued source of assessment information and an audience for assessment results (Shepard, Kagan, & Wirtz, 1998). Portfolios increase the effectiveness of teacher, student, and parent communication because portfolios provide directly observable products and understandable evidence concerning children's performance (Stiggins, 2005). For example, a child uses a portfolio during a child-involved conference with a parent to share perceptions of learning and collaboratively generate goals. Portfolios promote communication about a child's dispositions, growth, and achievement status at a point in time.

Teacher Effectiveness

In addition to instructional strategies that increase achievement, the teacher emerges as a key influence on children's level of achievement. Karoly (2005) concluded that programs with better trained caregivers are more effective. Research on teacher effectiveness documents what successful adults knew from personal experiences in schools: Skilled teachers create a positive effect on children's achievement and a positive and lasting effect on their lives. A teacher's enthusiasm for teaching and personal love of the subject matter is a model that motivates children and ultimately influences their achievement (Stronge, 2002). Young children are best nurtured in an encouraging and stimulating environment with a professional educator who is able to respond to the children's leads and needs (NAEYC & NAECS/SDE, 2003).

We know that high-quality early childhood programs and effective assessment systems rely upon well qualified and reflective teachers supported by ongoing inservice training (High/Scope Educational Research Foundation, 2005; Jones, 2003). One simple yet powerful example of professional development is teachers and administrators discussing and refining assessment together. Assessment decisions are enhanced when educators meet to build a consensus and common language, to agree on desired goals, and help standardize portfolio procedures and the assessment process (Jones, 2003).

Student Reflection and Self-Assessment

The development of children's self-assessment skills is a positive aspect of the portfolio process (Potter, 1999). It is possible and desirable to involve children in self-assessment and self-selection of products supported by their reflection on the learning that occurred. As Potter stated, "Helping children become more involved and responsible for their progress is consistent with a child-centered approach towards learning" (p. 210). Woodward (2000) considered it vital that children have a valid role in both their learning and the assessment of that learning. NAEYC and NAECS/SDE (2003) recommended that teachers involve children in evaluating their own work, and Black and William (1998) asserted that self-assessment is essential to any child's progress as a learner. Certainly, an important benefit of asking young students to reflect on their work is the opportunity it gives adults to learn about children's perspectives and value their participation in learning. Children are active partners in the classroom and are sincerely involved in assessment through their reflections and role in developing portfolios.

ASSESSMENT TERMS AND EXPLANATIONS

A list of explanations for key assessment terminology provides a succinct reference point for parents and educators to clarify applications. Customize this list to respond to staff assessment questions and to reflect the components in the school's assessment system. Share a list with parents to enhance communication.

Figure 1.2

Assessment Terms and Explanations

ASSESSMENT TERM	EXPLANATION
Assessment	Assessment is the continuous gathering and analysis of data to better understand individuals or groups. It is intended to provide feedback to children, families, and educators as well as diagnose and guide instruction. Tomlinson (1999) states that assessment is today's means of understanding how to modify tomorrow's instruction (p. 10).
Authentic assessment	Authentic assessment analyzes what a child actually does when learning. It evolves from meaningful, significant, and real learning tasks in natural learning environments. These tasks require children to generate responses rather than choose among descriptors, as in a force-choice response.
Authentic tasks	Authentic tasks are classroom learning experiences that resemble real life as closely as possible, such as a child making change in a play store rather than subtracting numbers on paper.
Benchmark	Benchmark is a synonym for an anchor product. A benchmark piece is an example of a student's work that is developmentally significant, denotes current targeted skills and concepts, and provides baseline data for later comparisons of how the child is changing as a learner.
Equitable	Assessments must be appropriate to the entire school population and provide a more objective standard in scoring and feedback so that assessment information is less subject to distortion, rater bias, and inconsistent expectations.
Learning profile	A child's learning profile is how that child best learns. It is influenced by prior experiences, age, gender, kinds of intelligences, culture, and learning modalities.
Learning standards	Learning standards communicate the essential skills and concepts at specific grade levels that children should know, understand, and be able to do.
Portfolio	A portfolio is a systematic collection representative of a child's work that the teacher and student select to provide information regarding each child's developmental readiness, learning profile, interests, achievement levels, and learning growth over time.
Readiness	Readiness is a child's preparedness to learn and is relative to the demands of the particular learning situation, understanding, and skill. It is influenced by age, prior experiences, and opportunities to learn.
Reliability	Reliability is the degree to which assessment tools and procedures yield dependable and consistent results.
Representative work	The products in a portfolio must be representative of the work typical of that child. Representative products reflect long-term patterns and trends in the child's learning and avoid isolated examples.

Assessment Terms and Explanations

ASSESSMENT TERM	EXPLANATION
Research-based	Research-based is a term stipulating that best practices evolve from a firm research foundation. Instruction and assessment decisions need to be evidenced-based rather than opinion-based. The terminology is used extensively in the No Child Left Behind legislation.
Rubric	A rubric is a guideline to quality and a standard for grading. It clarifies what quality looks like, and it is used to challenge children to think about quality work and how to plan for success. It is a scoring guide that delineates the criteria used to evaluate a product. It provides a clearer standard to determine grades more accurately and fairly.
School Career Portfolio	The School Career Portfolio is a selection of significant and representative items to document the child's accomplishments and levels of achievement over several years.
Showcase Portfolio	The School Career Portfolio is also referred to as a Showcase Portfolio since it focuses on a few selected products each year and is then added to each year to develop a long-term view of learning.
Validity	Validity indicates whether an assessment measures what it is intended to measure.
Yearly portfolio	The yearly portfolio is the accumulation of the products and reflections that represents each child's responses to the learning opportunities provided through the curriculum and learning standards. This portfolio is actively used throughout the school year, and then, the majority of the products are taken home as a keepsake.

2

Putting Portfolios Into Action

Portfolios are the heart of assessment with young children as they have the potential to recognize the uniqueness of each child while documenting the learning standards inherent in school programs. Children do not enter school with the same background experiences or profiles as learners, yet all are expected to achieve specified levels of learning. Portfolios are valued as a tool that focuses on both the affective and cognitive domains of children's learning while integrating learning standards throughout the curriculum.

"Portfolios promote success for children from all populations."

Portfolios offer a concrete record of children's modes of learning and the development of their talents and achievements during a year or more. In classrooms where all children develop portfolios, the process enables each student to be acknowledged for the level of work he or she produces. In this manner, portfolios promote students' success by providing multiple opportunities for children from every population to demonstrate talents and potential (Payne, 2003; Smutny, Walker, & Meckstroth, 2007). Portfolios assist teachers in their quest to honor the diversity of students and discover the strengths of each learner.

Portfolios are successfully used nationwide with children as young as four to celebrate children's work and validate their learning. Not everything a child produces is kept in the portfolio; rather, the portfolio is a selection of representative or especially significant items. Most of a child's work goes home on a regular basis so parents consistently see the fruits of their child's learning. This chapter provides information about using portfolios with young children by first defining what their portfolios are, then addressing how objectives for prekindergarten and kindergarten children differ from the objectives for first-through third-grade learners, and finally, outlining a sequence for implementing portfolios.

WHAT IS A PORTFOLIO?

> *"A portfolio is a systematic collection representative of a child's work that the teacher and student select to provide information regarding each child's developmental readiness, learning profile, interests, achievement levels, and learning growth over time."*

A significant concept in this definition is *systematic collection*. A systematic collection ensures that portfolios develop purposefully and continually by establishing when, how, and why products get into a portfolio, how it is managed, and what are its assessment applications. The products in a portfolio must be representative of the work that is typical of that child and not just the child's best work. Representative products reflect patterns and trends over a period in the child's learning and avoid isolated examples.

A second important concept in this definition is that both teacher-selected and child-selected products are incorporated. To document readiness levels, learning standards, and achievement, teachers determine which products are required portfolio pieces for all students. Then when appropriate, as children mature in their portfolio implementation, some products are child selected to individualize the portfolio, confirm interests, recognize students' ownership in the process, and motivate students' continued learning.

A vital concept in this definition is the use of the portfolio to document a child's learning profile and learning growth over time. Children and other invested individuals should review the portfolio to determine how each child is developing as a learner. Many children are more motivated to excel when they see for themselves that they are making progress and that their work is resulting in success. The goal is for portfolios to be educationally effective and personally satisfying for educators, children, and their families.

PORTFOLIO OBJECTIVES

Portfolio objectives develop and expand as children mature. The intent of portfolios with prekindergarten and kindergarten children is to initiate the portfolio process by involving children in collecting and managing a representative sample of work to document achievements and celebrate their learning. The intent with first- through third-grade children is to expand the portfolio process and increase students' involvement and responsibilities. Figure 2.1 elaborates on these objectives (Kingore, 2007).

Figure 2.1

Portfolio Objectives

Pre-K → K

1. **Develop students' feelings of self-worth.**
   When young children review their portfolios, they see products to compare over time and realize that their skills are increasing. They feel important and successful.

2. **Use repeated tasks to document each child's level of learning standards, growth, and achievements.**
   Repeated tasks document the children's achievement level of learning standards by substantiating children's increased integration of concepts and skills over time. Children, parents, other educators, and administrators benefit from viewing products that exemplify the pace and level of each child's learning.

3. **Document learning and determine effective instructional accommodations.**
   The work children produce confirms their learning and encourages appropriate instruction to be initiated in a timely fashion. Products from authentic learning experiences in a classroom are valuable components to align with other data when diagnosing young students with learning differences or special needs as well as students who would benefit from extended learning opportunities.

4. **Celebrate learning.**
   Children review their portfolios to celebrate their learning accomplishments; they delight in sharing with others what they have learned and what they are currently able to do. Parents review their child's portfolio to concretely understand and celebrate the learning growth of their child.

Grades 1 → 3

1. **Develop students' feelings of self-worth.**
   As they review their portfolios over time, primary children develop feelings of self-worth and observe concrete indications of their growth and changes as learners. They substantiate to themselves that their efforts result in achievement.

2. **Teach young children to manage, organize, and file their portfolio products.**
   Typically, young children are not organized. Organization and management are valued

life skills children must develop over time. A simple but clearly structured portfolio system helps children learn how to organize, manage, and maintain their work.

3. **Increase children's responsibility for learning.**
   The portfolio process requires children to analyze their learning rather than rely only on the evaluations of others. They are responsible for reviewing several pieces of their work to select portfolio products supported by their reflection upon their learning and achievement.

4. **Use repeated tasks to document each child's level of learning standards, growth, and achievements.**
   Repeated tasks document the achievement of learning standards by substantiating children's increased integration of concepts and skills over time. Children, parents, other educators, and administrators benefit from viewing products that exemplify the pace and level of each child's learning.

5. **Document readiness levels and determine learning goals.**
   The work students produce confirms readiness, augments understanding of information from standardized evaluations, and forms a foundation for collaborative goal setting. Products document the level at which concepts and skills are attained by primary students with fewer skills, students on grade level, students with learning differences or special needs, and students who would benefit from extended learning opportunities. The portfolio is a concrete means to demonstrate achievements related to placement in special classes or to encourage that appropriate intervention is initiated in a timely fashion.

6. **Implement effective self-assessment and collaborative evaluation.**
   Many students talk about grades as something given to them by teachers. Self-assessment is clearly needed to promote students' reflection about what they have earned by their effort. Well-developed criteria, often shared in the form of holistic or analytical rubrics, stimulate students' self assessments and lead to collaborative evaluations between teachers and students as they consider the merits and demerits of a product or process.

7. **Celebrate learning and share information with others.**
   Children review their portfolios to acknowledge their learning accomplishment. When viewed over time, portfolios promote students' celebrations of learning and enable them to share evidence of learning with family, the teacher, and peers. Children can also present their learning achievements through student-involved conferences.

8. **Document district and state learning standards.**
   Portfolio products document learning standards by substantiating students' application of concepts and skills. Teachers' and students' reflections can specifically address the standards inherent in the product.

PLANNING A SEQUENCE FOR IMPLEMENTING PORTFOLIOS

Effective portfolios are not a lucky accident, and effective teachers do not rely on spontaneous moments when wonderful products develop and children rush to their portfolios to include the new treasure. Taking time to plan increases the likelihood of success and prevents frustration later. Design a sequence for implementing portfolios by prioritizing, organizing, communicating, and integrating (Kingore, 2007).

Prioritize

- To develop a plan for schoolwide implementation of portfolios, work as a group to address the prompts posed as staff discussion questions in Figure 2.2.
- To develop a portfolio plan for your classroom only, use the discussion questions in Figure 2.2 to promote your decision making.
- Decide the number and kind of products you want in the portfolios.
- Avoid attempting too much at one time. Prioritize so you can begin small and let the process develop with time and experience.
- Allow the portfolios to reflect the personal goals, styles, strengths, and needs of you and your class.

Figure 2.2

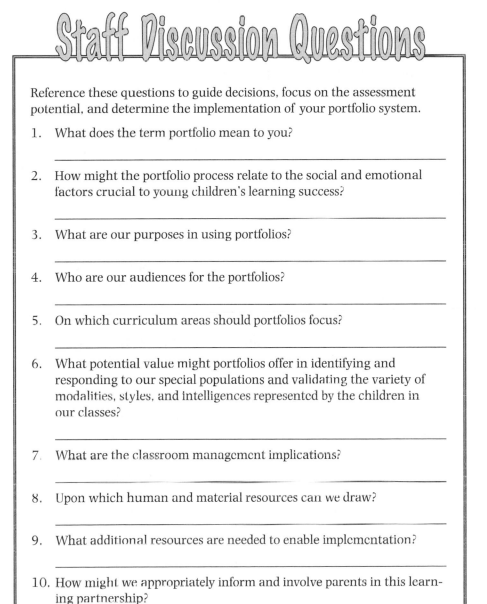

Staff Discussion Questions

Reference these questions to guide decisions, focus on the assessment potential, and determine the implementation of your portfolio system.

1. What does the term portfolio mean to you?

2. How might the portfolio process relate to the social and emotional factors crucial to young children's learning success?

3. What are our purposes in using portfolios?

4. Who are our audiences for the portfolios?

5. On which curriculum areas should portfolios focus?

6. What potential value might portfolios offer in identifying and responding to our special populations and validating the variety of modalities, styles, and intelligences represented by the children in our classes?

7. What are the classroom management implications?

8. Upon which human and material resources can we draw?

9. What additional resources are needed to enable implementation?

10. How might we appropriately inform and involve parents in this learning partnership?

Organize

- Determine the portfolio containers, storage location, and management procedures. (Chapter 3 discusses suggestions to guide organization and management.)
- Organize a process and schedule for selecting portfolio products.
- Organize an ongoing schedule for when children's work goes home and communicate that schedule to parents.
- Prepare needed forms and assemble needed materials.
- Plan the first item for students to file in their portfolio so the process begins smoothly and quickly. For example, determine a specific repeated task for students to complete and file as soon as portfolios are implemented. (Chapter 5 includes a discussion of repeated tasks and suggests several applications.)

Communicate

Communicate With Other Teachers and Administrators

- Network with other interested educators to nurture ideas and successes as you share concerns or problems.
- Brainstorm whether there is an easier way to do this.
- Begin an ongoing need-to-know list with questions that occur to you so that you can network with and learn from other professionals using portfolios.
- Share articles, books, and information about portfolios.

Communicate With Families

- Send letters to families every month to share information about children's progress and their use of portfolios. (Chapter 6 includes several sample letters to families.)
- Conduct meetings with parents during which you model portfolios, discuss the process, have children share their portfolios, and note the growth and pride the children demonstrate. Emphasize to families that portfolios provide concrete examples to revisit over time in order to understand the capabilities, achievements, and potential of children. (Chapter 6 elaborates multiple ideas for productive meetings and communications with families.)
- Develop a file folder of brief articles and information regarding the use of portfolios and authentic assessments to offer family members who have questions about the process. Consider including the list of assessment terms and explanations shared in Chapter 1.

Communicate With Children

- Show children what a portfolio is and explain how they will use one in class.
- Discuss how older students use portfolios for job interviews and college entrances. Explain how some adults use portfolios for job advancement

or to obtain a new job. When possible, invite older students or adults to share their portfolios with the children and explain why portfolios are important and useful in their lives.

- Discuss the children's ownership and pride. Explain how they will be responsible for filing and organizing their work, just as adults do in their jobs.

Connecting Learning Experience

A Think Aloud About Portfolios

A *think aloud* is a metacognitive strategy to model a thinking process verbally with children. Think out loud about the potential personal value of portfolios for children and verbalize your thinking with the class. The objective is to use your perspective to ignite children's enthusiasm to begin their portfolios. The following is one example of a think aloud.

> *"As I look at you now, I am thinking about how your portfolios will look many days from now. Your portfolio will become the finest book you have ever developed. It will show others some of the most important things you learn and the things that are most important to you. You will get to keep your portfolio forever. When you get older, you can look through your portfolio and celebrate your learning."*

Integrate

Portfolios should reflect instructional decisions and authentic learning experiences in a class. Looking through a child's portfolio reveals a clear view of instructional priorities and the kinds of learning experiences most often provided. Strive to make portfolios a part of the regular routine in your class rather than something extra to do.

- Establish a specific time for portfolio product selection and maintain your schedule. Do not leave it to chance.
- Integrate portfolios into children's learning experiences by involving them in the filing and management of their portfolio products. Chapter 3 offers several management suggestions for young children.
- Set aside time for giving children feedback and for developing the portfolio and its components.

Share criteria for quality work and, as appropriate, ask children to review their portfolio and choose something they did well to share with a classmate or family member.

- Integrate portfolios with assessment goals and topic objectives. Review the children's portfolios to document learning accomplishments and guide instructional pacing.
- Integrate portfolios with instructional decisions. How do portfolios showcase the kind of instructional experiences that best benefit students? How do portfolios support the effectiveness of a wide array of learning tasks beyond simple fill-in-the-blank responses?
- Connect portfolio products to children's capabilities and potential. Integrate multiple modalities and/or intelligences in the product opportunities available to students.

3

Child-Involved Portfolio Management

Rather than view portfolios as a teacher responsibility or project, a more productive perspective of portfolios with young children views the teacher as a facilitator establishing an effective, child-involved portfolio system. When children are significantly involved in the ongoing organization and management, portfolios are more likely to increase pride in their work and extend their intrinsic motivation to learn. First, introduce the process of developing portfolios to the children. Then, keep the materials inexpensive and the organization and management process simple enough that children can maintain most of the portfolio themselves, thereby freeing teachers from additional paper management.

INTRODUCING THE PROCESS TO YOUNG CHILDREN

Modeling a portfolio can inspire children's interest in developing their own portfolios. People typically smile as they share the items in their portfolio and their personal pride of accomplishment shines through. Consider using one or more of these modeling options.

If You and This Year's Students Have Previously Developed Portfolios

- Have each child select one product from last year's portfolio to share with the class as an introduction to him- or herself and his or her achievements.
- Have the children discuss what they like about their portfolios. Elicit their suggestions for making portfolios even better this year.
- Together, develop a class list of possible criteria to guide the selection of portfolio items. Ask, "What should we think about when we select a product for our portfolios?"

Oral Presentations With Products

The School Career Portfolio (discussed in Chapter 7) affords a valuable language experience at the beginning of the school year. Ask each child to choose one piece from this portfolio to share with the new class as a personal introduction. This special show-and-tell is a rich oral language experience and invites children to talk about themselves and promote the idea that each of them is unique, important, and knowledgeable. Having the child presenting the product shows that he or she is truly the only one who knows the information that is shared.

If You Have Previously Implemented Portfolios in Your Classes But This Year's Children Have Not

- Invite two to four children from last year's class to show and discuss their portfolios with this year's students. This panel can highlight the process and how they feel about portfolios.
- Emphasize how individual and different portfolios are because each reflects personal strengths and choices.
- Encourage this year's class to ask questions.

If You and Your Students Have Not Previously Developed Portfolios

- Make portfolios as concrete as possible so children understand what a portfolio looks like, the reasons they will be developing one, and what benefits it provides.
- Put together and bind a collection of children's work to create a mock-up of how portfolios may look. Explain to them that they will take many papers home to show their family but keep a few papers at school to combine into a wonderful book to amaze their family at the end of the year. The intent is to get the children excited about creating their own portfolios.
- Have a significant adult visitor such as the principal or a parent briefly talk with the class about how wonderful it will be to have this portfolio book at the end of the school year. Discuss together how the children can look back through their portfolios when they are older and remember this year of school and the important things they learned.

Show children how and where their portfolios will be stored in the classroom. Then children decorate a folder to create their portfolio container and place it in the storage area. Immediately after discussing the process, build enthusiasm for the portfolio process by having children produce the first product for them to file in their portfolio such as drawing a picture of their family and then dictating or writing about it.

MATERIALS

The checklist in Figure 3.1 can be used to record a list of needed materials and forms to duplicate. Keep the list short and inexpensive so cost does not impede the process.

Figure 3.1 Materials Checklist

Materials:
- ☐ Digital camera or conventional camera and film
- ☐ Crate, box, or file drawer to store class portfolios
- ☐ Folders: pocket folders or expandable folders—one per child
- ☐ Hanging files—one per child
- ☐ Stapler
- ☐ Sticky notes
- ☐ _____
- ☐ _____
- ☐ _____
- ☐ _____

Forms to duplicate: Page/Figure:
- ☐ _____   _____
- ☐ _____   _____
- ☐ _____   _____
- ☐ _____   _____
- ☐ _____   _____

Optional:
- ☐ Audiotapes and tape recorder
- ☐ Computers, computer-generated products
- ☐ Date stamp
- ☐ Timer
- ☐ Videotapes and access to a video camera
- ☐ _____
- ☐ _____
- ☐ _____
- ☐ _____

ORGANIZING THE PROCESS

Production—Collection—Selection—Reflection

The basic portfolio process involves production, collection, selection, and reflection. Collect the work children produce over a few days. Periodically select a piece that represents a segment of learning and key standards. Then teachers (and later children) reflect on each selection to clarify its significance to everyone who views the products.

Name + Date + Caption

Every piece in a portfolio includes three things: a child's name, the date, and a caption stapled on the product. The child's name is an obvious necessity, and when children write their names by themselves, it becomes a simple visual that substantiates handwriting and fine-motor development. Any stage of scribbling or creative spelling can communicate that child's name as long as it is recognizable to the child. The date is included to document the progression of skills and the child's learning growth over time. A date stamp is easily used, or most young children can copy the number for the date if it is provided for them on the chalkboard. The caption clarifies the incorporated skills and concepts, reflects feelings about the work, and encourages self-assessment.

Teachers new to using portfolios may wonder if it would be simpler to omit the reflective statements when the portfolio process is initiated with young children. It seems easier to have one less thing to manage as you begin. If possible, however, incorporate reflective statements from the very start. Reflections increase children's involvement in the process and provide a window to their perspectives (NAEYC & NAECS/SDE, 2003; Potter, 1999; Woodward, 2000). Products without reflections have less significance over time. When families, teachers, or even students look back on portfolio products without a caption, it is more difficult to connect specific learning objectives and understand or value the importance of each piece. The reward for incorporating self-assessments and reflections is that children, families, and teachers gain an increased awareness of the child's perspective, patterns of learning strengths, and dispositions toward learning.

Some teachers prefer to complete the organization and management of the portfolios for the children. These teachers feel most secure when they organize and file the portfolio products themselves. Most teachers, however, affirm that even four- and five-year-olds can complete much of the management once the teacher plans an organization process that is developmentally appropriate for each age group. Children demonstrate pleasure and feelings of importance as they prepare and file their products. An added benefit is reduced paperwork for the teacher—when children manage the portfolio, teachers gain classroom time to complete other tasks. Consider the following ideas to organize the portfolio process appropriately in an early childhood or primary classroom.

1. Very young children can successfully file their own products when teachers plan portfolios in a developmentally appropriate manner. A plastic crate with hanging files is a great choice for portfolios that young children manage. Place the hanging files in the crate (or box or file drawer) and locate the files in an area accessible to the children.

2. Photograph each child. On each hanging file, write a child's name and staple or glue the child's photograph to the hanging file so that it extends above the top of the file and so that it is easily seen. Placing photographs on each file allows young children to successfully locate

their portfolios and file their own work even if they cannot recognize their names. Small photographs are more durable when glued or stapled to a popsicle stick and each stick stapled to a hanging file so that the photo extends above the top of the file.

3. Each child uses crayons, markers, or paint to personalize and decorate a pocket folder or expandable file folder as a portfolio container. Write the child's name on the decorated container and have the child place it in the hanging file displaying the child's photograph. The decorated file folder becomes the portfolio container; the hanging file is the organizer that maintains the place for each portfolio. Using a file folder as the portfolio container allows children to take their portfolios out of the hanging files without mixing up the organization or sequence of the entire filing system in the crate.

4. Establish specific times for children to select and file products in portfolios to ensure that the desired number and range of items is included. For example, many classes have children take several days' work home on the same day each week so parents know when to expect and review their child's papers. As a part of the portfolio system, children file a specific product in the portfolio before taking the rest of that week's work home.

Young students manage their own filing best when the products in the portfolios are organized chronologically. Teach children to slide the products forward in their portfolio each time and then place their newest selections in the back of their portfolio. By filing in the back, the portfolio remains generally in chronological order. Furthermore, each time students file a product they see their earlier work to compare with what they are now able to do. This comparison becomes a concrete reminder of how much they are learning, and young children particularly benefit from being able to view their progress clearly over time.

Role-play filing papers into a portfolio so young children can see the process. Model sliding the products forward in the file to make room to place the newest work in the back of the folder. Stress how important filing is and that the children will be filing papers just as older students and adults organize their work.

Create an atmosphere of celebration when it is time to file the first products in the portfolios. It is fun to shake hands and congratulate children as they file their first papers. Invite children to write a note informing families about the occasion or to duplicate simple notes such as Figure 3.2 to send home to share this important beginning with the children's families. Children can illustrate the note, draw their faces to show how they feel, and write their names at the bottom of the note. It is fascinating how much children enjoy completing their own filing; it makes them feel more grown-up and affirms that their work is important.

Figure 3.2 Filing Note

Date _____

Dear Family,

I am starting a portfolio of my work. I get to add new things to it all year to show you what I am learning. Today, I filed my first paper in my portfolio. This is how I feel.

Love,

As children acquire several products in their portfolios, have them or an adult use a pencil to number the products lightly in their portfolio in sequential order. Then, if an item drops out, it is more easily returned to the correct place.

These procedures combine with adults' enthusiasm about the portfolio process to increase young children's excitement about their portfolios and move them to ask repeatedly if it is time to file more of their work. Create a small picture symbol for the portfolios such as a picture of a portfolio folder and tape that picture on a date on the class calendar to show children when it is time for product selection and filing. Then move the symbol ahead to the next selection date each time children complete portfolio selection.

A class portfolio is an additional component to build into the portfolio process, particularly in second- and third-grade classrooms. Children and the teacher collaboratively assemble works that reflect the achievements and projects of the class as a whole. The class portfolio becomes a collective scrapbook or database in which all of the students participate and gain ownership in the learning process as they celebrate completed tasks and occasions. It is typically contained in a photo album in which weekly entries in the form of pictures, words, and work samples are made to herald the content and learning experiences of the class.

Children take turns serving as the class historian for one week who makes choices about what to include and record to represent the learning topics, skills, and events of that week in class. Eventually, every child should have the opportunity to serve as the class historian. A class portfolio is a special opportunity for children to select work and reflect upon learning accomplishments as a community of learners rather than only as individuals. Over time, it becomes a memory scrapbook with assessment potential as it represents the curriculum and class experiences for the entire year.

REFLECTION AS A TEACHER-DIRECTED LEARNING TASK

Particularly in kindergarten and first grade, reflection can be used as a language arts activity during the week when selection occurs. In a teacher-directed, small group setting, the teacher works with one group each day and writes those children's dictations. The teacher prompts children's thinking with one or more inquiry probes and statements that help them reflect on their work.

- Tell me about your picture.
- Tell me about your work.
- Tell me more so I understand your ideas.
- What was your favorite part?
- What did you think was easy to do?
- What was the hardest thing to do?
- How did you figure this out?

As the teacher takes dictations from one student, the others can share their products with each other, complete an independent language arts task, or work with manipulatives such as word puzzles or alphabet tasks. Thus the teacher is able to individualize instruction and complete four to six reflections each day instead of trying to work with a whole class at one time.

SIZE OF A PORTFOLIO

"A portfolio is a file, not a pile."

Portfolios do not need to be large to accomplish the objectives stated in Chapter 2. Portfolios that are too large create storage problems and may reflect attempts to save some *stuff* rather than a planned system with assessment potential.

How many products are needed in a portfolio? While there is no absolute number, it is helpful to think of a portfolio as a file not a pile. It is a *selection* of representative work rather than a *collection* of everything that has been done. Portfolios for young children can be relatively small and still result in a means to document learning and provide a tremendous source of pride for children and families.

> *"Think of an inch or less for each child's portfolio as you determine how much storage room you may need."*

For prekindergarten and kindergarten levels, teachers plan a one-fourth-inch to one-half-inch thickness as the total size per portfolio for the year. Young children produce fewer paper products since much of the learning completed by this age group is process oriented. The teacher plans one product selection every two or three weeks to ensure that the desired number of items and range of skills, concepts, and content areas are included. After the teacher and children discuss a product to save in the portfolio, the children write their names on a caption strip to attach to the product that lists the learning task and the incorporated skills. (Refer to skill captions in Chapter 5 for examples and an elaboration of this feature.) The children can also write or dictate more elaborated ideas about the work. Each child then files that selection in the portfolio. If systematically collected throughout the year, this relatively small sample of twelve to eighteen products effectively documents the growth and changes in the abilities of these children.

For first- through third-grade levels, plan a one-half-inch to one-inch thickness as the total size per portfolio for the year. Incorporate a collaborative selection approach in which both the teacher and children are actively involved in selecting portfolio items. Children select a product every one or two weeks to file in portfolios as documentation of learning achievements and interests; the teacher selects one product every three weeks or so to ensure that a representative range of skills, concepts, and content areas are included. In each case, children write their names and reflections on a caption strip to attach to the product before it is filed in the portfolio. If systematically collected throughout the year, this collaborative approach results in a portfolio with thirty or more products documenting the achievement levels of curriculum learning standards and the personal choices and accomplishments of the individual children.

WHO SELECTS THE PRODUCTS?

In order for a portfolio to have potential assessment value and a clear record of the progression of skills and concepts, teachers must designate several products to be included in every child's portfolio. This menu of required products elevates the portfolio from a *best works* file to a systematic documentation of achieved skill levels in relationship to required learning standards.

> *"A portfolio is not a collection of best work. Rather, it is documentation of learning achievements and learning changes over time."*

In order for a portfolio to reflect the individuality and uniqueness of each child, children need to be responsible for selecting several products representing their interests and accomplishments. When children have a role in the selection process, the portfolios are more personally valued by each child and become as varied as the children.

"Young children's portfolios should be as varied and unique as the children themselves."

Some teachers have successfully involved very young children in the selection process from the start, while other teachers report that prekindergarten and kindergarten children have difficulty making selections and dictating captions early in the year. They note that the process can be excessive due to the age of the children and the time it takes to complete the selection and reflection. When the difficulties of selection and reflection process outweigh the values, the teacher can initially determine which products go in the portfolios while still involving children in the reflection process as a teacher-directed learning experience. Begin to incorporate some of the ideas suggested in the next section.

As soon as it is appropriate, more actively involve children in the decision-making process. As early as the second half of kindergarten and certainly by first grade, children should assume a substantial role in product selection for their portfolios. Significant advantages result when children review a few products to decide which one to include. Typically, children

- apply high-level thinking as they analyze alternatives;
- practice decision making;
- begin to develop self-assessment skills;
- assume some responsibility for their learning;
- perceive a more concrete overview of their developing skills and concepts;
- delight in their accomplishments and/or challenge themselves to higher achievements;
- engage in goal setting.

When children are active partners in product selection, they have more ownership in their portfolios. The portfolio is not something someone else is doing. Children begin to use personal pronouns as they discuss the portfolios and share products with others. Statements such as "Look what I did," "This was a hard problem but I figured it out," and "My spelling is really getting better" are heard as young children select a product and informally discuss their portfolios with peers.

INCREASING CHILDREN'S ROLE IN SELECTION AND REFLECTION

When appropriate in the kindergarten through third-grade years, increase children's higher order thinking and ownership in the portfolio process by increasing their involvement in selection choice and reflection. One initial approach is to collect two products for each child. Duplicate copies of a simple caption card such as one of the four samples in Figures 3.3 to 3.6 that states the criterion you want children to focus on for this product. Meet with the children, usually in small groups but individually if preferred, and state the criterion such as "Select a product you liked doing." Ask each child to choose one of the two products to file in their portfolio. Encourage children to write their names and even draw or write reflections on the duplicated caption card while they wait turns filing products. An adult or the child staples the caption card to the product before it is filed in the portfolio. This approach is continued as needed over several weeks until children are ready for an increased role in selection and reflection.

Connecting Learning Experience

A Task for Buddies

Buddies are older students who work with younger children to complete a learning task. Teachers recognize that buddies aid children's affective, social, and cognitive development. Usually in one-to-one settings, a buddy can assist a child during the selection process and record dictation on a reflective caption or facilitate as the child writes the caption. When the buddies work together, the teacher moves among the children to facilitate and assess by writing notes or completing a checklist of observations.

In the spirit of cooperative learning, buddies can bring one of their products to share and discuss with the younger children. The teacher brainstorms in advance with the young students to prepare questions they can ask as they interact with their buddies.

With experience, children can consider more than two product alternatives when selecting portfolio products. To model and guide the selection and reflection process, structure the parameters by narrowing the choices to a specific content such as three writing samples. Then state the criterion for children to consider as they review the items such as "Select a product that shows how you are getting better in your writing. How is your writing improving?" Children have some choice but do not feel overwhelmed because they are working within the parameters established by the teacher. Each child selects one of the three items and completes a caption reflecting upon that choice. This approach is continued as needed.

Next increase the frequency of students' selections and reflections. After several successful experiences, students can select a portfolio piece every one or two weeks from two or more collected items. At this point, children are practicing analysis and evaluation skills as they think about their work and increase their ownership in the product selection process. Most beginning writers use simple caption strips to complete a reflection about a product for their portfolios. The teacher can add elaborations dictated by those children not ready to write more than a word or two. Student buddies from upper-elementary classrooms can also be used as scribes to assist children in recording or embellishing their reflections.

Eventually, the entire class can be involved in product selection at the same time with each child reviewing work from several days and determining which product to select. At this point, selection and reflection evolves into a collaborative approach with some portfolio items determined by the teachers and some products freely selected by the children. Criteria are expanded to encourage a deepening of children's evaluative thinking and evidence both strengths and goals. Prompt children's thinking by stating "Select a piece that you want to tell someone about" or "Select something that you did well and tell why."

Figure 3.3 Caption Cards

Figure 3.4 Caption Cards

Figure 3.5 Caption Cards

Figure 3.6 Caption Cards

Four sample caption cards in Figures 3.3 to 3.6 are designed to duplicate, cut apart, and use one at a time. The cards allow a comfortable, open space for children to write their names, words, or even a reflective sentence without worrying about exact letter formation between handwriting lines. The picture prompts on each card help children comprehend and remember what the criterion states after the teacher has read it to them.

Another version of a simple reflection tool to use with young children is the check box format in Figures 3.7 and 3.8. This variation presents two criteria statements. The teacher or children read the two options and each child checks the one or two statements he or she chooses as a reflection. The rest of the space on the form allows room for drawing, writing words, or writing a reflective sentence about the work. These captions are designed flexibly so students can write a response choosing to use the handwriting lines if they prefer. The choice is important because some primary teachers report better success for children when they use caption strips without lines.

Figure 3.7 Caption Check Boxes

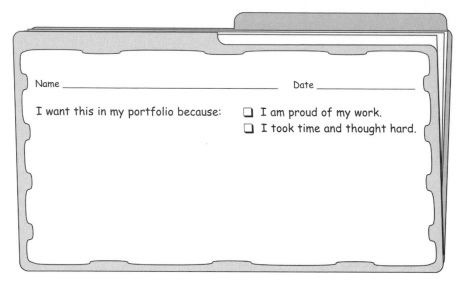

Figure 3.8 Caption Check Boxes

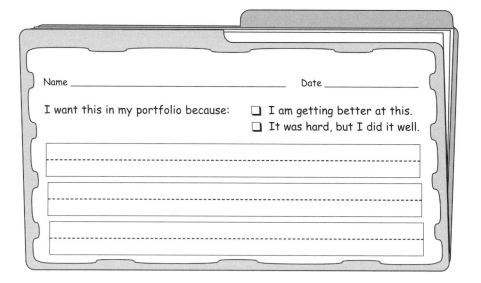

Avoid using best work as a criterion for prekindergarten through first-grade students. That criterion is value laden and judgmental; young children are generally not ready to compare or contrast to determine what is best. Using the term *best work* leads children to ask adults what they think is best or to select only products with high grades on them. It also encourages some children to verbalize negative comparisons such as "Mine is not as good as yours." Children react more comfortably and positively to criteria such as those listed in the captions in this chapter.

A PORTFOLIO CENTER

Some teachers find it useful to incorporate a portfolio management center as one of the ongoing centers in the room. This center consists of a small desk or table that stores the portfolios and all of the supplies needed to complete additions to portfolios such as copies of blank caption forms, pencils, markers, and a stapler. Children go to the center to complete their reflections and file their selection. A displayed chart such as Figure 3.9 provides an authentic literacy experience and guides children so they can complete the process independently.

Connecting Learning Experience

Developing a Class Portfolio Center

As an authentic planning and language arts activity, work with the children to create a class portfolio center. Brainstorm together which materials and supplies are needed as you discuss procedures for using the center. Elicit the children's ideas and help them sequence the process. Finalize the discussion by organizing their ideas on a chart to post in the center that guides their application. Developing the chart as a class develops their understanding and promotes additional ownership in the process.

Figure 3.9 Portfolio Chart

Connecting Learning Experience

Creating a Word Bank

Expand the literacy experience of a portfolio center by including a poster of words and phrases that express children's feelings and reactions to their products such as *happy, good, important work,* or *I used my brain.* As a class, brainstorm which words and ideas children want to list and write those words in large print on a poster or chart paper to display in the portfolio center. Over time, add words to the poster when children express a new idea: "We should add that to our poster."

These word prompts are invitations for children to integrate reading and writing skills at different levels of complexity as they complete caption forms in the center. Many children are pleased to write just their name and then draw a face on the caption form to show how they feel about this work. Others might refer to the word bank and select one or more words to copy on their captions. Still other children may decide to write their own words in their temporary spelling.

WORDS OF EXPERIENCE

To guide educators who are beginning the portfolio process, teachers across the nation were asked to share advice and ideas for simplicity and success. This collage of ideas presents some of the most frequent suggestions from teachers in prekindergarten through third grade who implemented portfolios and authentic assessment (Kingore, 2007).

"I never thought kindergartners could do all this. They are so proud of themselves when they file their papers or share a portfolio product with someone."

"Most of our first year, we just kept worrying if we were doing it all right. Our advice is to relax and learn along with the students what parts work best in your classes."

"Product selection for portfolios worked best with my little ones when we did it in small groups. They enjoyed the more individual attention. I had some children in the small group share their products with each other while I worked with one or two children and wrote captions. After once or twice, it proceeded smoothly and worked well."

"Portfolios are a self-esteem boost for the special-needs students in my inclusion class. They see they are doing better each time we review the portfolio products."

"I assess the portfolios to assure that my advanced-level students reach an appropriate level of depth and complexity. Their products should demonstrate and document all their areas of advanced potential."

"I found that my enthusiasm for the process was infectious to students and parents!"

"The more I observe and use authentic assessments with my students, the better I understand them as individuals."

"My special education students in my mixed-ability class always smile when they review their portfolios. They could see that other children did work differently and that was still okay. In my classroom, it helped kids get over that idea that there was only one way to be right."

"Attaching children's photographs to their portfolios was a huge success with my class! It increased children's independence and simplified management. They love it."

"Let young students keep a small number of sticky notes in their work folder. The children use a sticky note to flag a paper they want in their portfolio so they are ready to dictate their reflective caption to an older student or adult scribe."

"As children survey their collection of work to select a piece for their portfolio, you get a clear view of your teaching priorities and the kinds of learning tasks you've been providing. I'm a better teacher because I am using the portfolio for my assessment, too."

"I think one of the most amazing things to me was how supportive the parents have been. They seem really impressed with what their kids know about their own learning."

"Rather than feel as if you have to do it all, plan for the year and set realistic goals for yourself according to your level of experience with portfolios (beginner, intermediate, or advanced)."

"I would like to plan a time for my class to share their portfolios with their friends in another class. My class is the only second grade class using portfolios and it might encourage other teachers to try it."

4

Products That Impact Assessment

Products document children's achievement of learning objectives and provide concrete evidence of their learning. Hence products impact assessment in multiple ways.

- As students work on a product task, teachers assess children's processes by observing work habits and both verbal and nonverbal responses.
- Completed products confirm children's levels of understanding.
- Teachers assess completed products to monitor and adjust instruction and to ensure that all children experience continuous learning success.
- Products become an evaluation tool when teachers evaluate the quality of the products and assign grades.
- Over time, children, families, and teachers can use products in a portfolio to assess how a child is changing as a learner.

In effective portfolios, the products are an integral reflection of the curriculum and of what children learn rather than a random collection of activities and isolated skills. Attention to authentic and meaningful learning tasks is a crucial consideration when selecting a menu of portfolio products. This chapter includes criteria to evaluate the effectiveness of potential portfolio products and compares the application of open-ended and single-correct-answer products. Teachers can skim a chart of potential portfolio products applicable to multiple content areas to prompt their decisions regarding the most appropriate products to use to assess and document children's abilities as well as showcase learning growth.

PRODUCT CRITERIA

Learning experiences and products in effective classrooms are much more than just something for children to do. Product decisions are based upon instructional objectives that facilitate children's learning growth. The reason to select a product is that it supports the children's learning and effectively substantiates their responses to targeted learning skills or concepts. Early childhood teachers seek products that attract, intrigue, excite, absorb, and actively involve children in wanting to complete learning tasks. They also request learning tasks with less writing so children's hands do not wear out before their heads. Consider the following criteria when planning items to include in portfolios.

Effective Portfolio Products

- Include developmentally appropriate options that match instructional priorities and children's learning profiles.
- Result from authentic learning experiences that apply strategies proven through research to have the highest effect on achievement.
- Document the level of learning for one or more targeted learning objectives or standards.
- Promote success and continuous learning for all children.
- Incorporate an array of learning tasks beyond simple fill-in-the-blank responses to encompass multiple modalities and encourage different levels of complexity.
- Promote high levels of thinking.
- Promote respect for student differences rather than label children as more or less able.
- Promote mental and process engagement.

The classroom teacher or teaching team continually questions to ensure that instruction results in the most productive and developmentally appropriate opportunities for children.

- Is this a learning opportunity most children should experience?
- Is this an important and authentic task for children to complete?
- Is the potential effect worth the instructional investment in time?

Incorporate these criteria and questions to reach decisions regarding which learning tasks promise the greatest potential for long-term learning and high achievement. Prioritize preferred criteria and then use Figure 4.1 to list product criteria and evaluate potential products in relation to those criteria. As one application, use a plus (+) or minus (–) to efficiently and simply evaluate each criterion for specific products. However, when a weighted evaluation is desired, appraise each criterion for a product on a scale of one to five with *one* earning a low value and *five* earning a high value. In the example shared here, a team of first-grade teachers and administrators uses the product criteria grid to reach a consensus regarding the merits and concerns of certain products in their curriculum. After discussion, they effectively prioritized which products to use most frequently.

Figure 4.1 Completed Product Criteria Grid

CRITERIA (Score each from 5 to 1 — 5 = Highly valued, 1 = Low value · OR · Score a + or – — + = Highly valued, – = Low value) — PRODUCTS	Learning logs	Charts/graphic organizers	Math story problems	Tests/quizzes	Dictations	Drawings/sketches
Developmentally appropriate	5	4	4	3	5	5
Matches instructional priorities and children's learning profiles	5	3	4	2	4	5
Results from an authentic learning experience	5	5	3	3	5	5
Applies research-based strategies	5	4	3	3	5	5
Documents learning for targeted objectives or standards	5	5	5	5	4	4
Promotes success and continuous learning	5	4	4	3	5	4
Incorporates multiple modalities and levels of complexity	5	4	4	2	4	4
Promotes high levels of thinking	5	5	5	3	5	4
Promotes respect	5	3	3	3	5	3
Promotes mental and process engagement	5	3	4	2	5	5

Continued on next page.

Score each from 5 to 1
   5 = Highly valued
   1 = Low value

· OR ·

   Score a + or −
   + = Highly valued
   − = Low value

CRITERIA

PRODUCTS

OPEN-ENDED AND SINGLE-CORRECT-ANSWER PRODUCTS

Research supports the effectiveness of teachers providing a wide array of learning tasks beyond simple fill-in-the-blank responses (Hertzog, 1998; High/Scope Educational Research Foundation, 2005; NAEYC, 1997). Single-correct-answer responses are more limiting in the modalities and levels of thinking that they encourage children to apply and thus risk lowering the opportunity for high-level responses from some children. To ensure opportunities for success and high achievement from all children, select portfolio products that result from both single-correct-answer and open-ended tasks. Open-ended does not mean *easy* or that all answers are correct. It means that more than one answer and more than one procedure are possible, encouraging children to bring their individuality to each learning opportunity. Hence open-ended tasks allow more children to be successful by honoring diverse modalities, ideas, and processes rather than rewarding only simple memorized answers.

Open-Ended Tasks

- Celebrate diversity in thinking by encouraging children to respond with multiple correct ideas at different levels of understanding.
- Honor different responses and different ways of learning by allowing a better match to children's preferred mode of learning.
- Encourage active participation and challenge children to generate responses.
- Integrate high-level thinking as the open-ended nature of these tasks challenge children to apply, analyze, synthesize, and evaluate.
- Adapt to multiple concepts and topics of study.

As typical of effective learning experiences with young children, open-ended experiences are introduced through teacher-directed instruction and modeling. Children cannot work independently until they have experienced success and are certain how to complete the tasks. Teachers include both simple and more complex product samples for comparison so children view a range of ways to succeed.

Open-ended tasks are not appropriate in all learning situations. Early childhood teachers determine when to provide multiple open-ended opportunities to promote high achievement for all children. Compare several learning experiences in Figure 4.2 as examples of tasks that promote open-ended or single answer products.

Figure 4.2 A Comparison of Open-Ended and Single-Answer Products

OPEN-ENDED PRODUCT EXAMPLES	SINGLE-CORRECT-ANSWER PRODUCT EXAMPLES
To complete a performance task, a child uses provided recyclable items to make a simple machine and explain its function.	To complete a test, a child marks the correct terms used in simple machines.
On an individual chalkboard or paper, a child shows three different ways to solve an addition problem.	On an individual chalkboard or paper, a child writes the answers to math addition problems.
Children use words and illustrations on a Venn diagram to compare similarities and differences between two key characters in a story.	A child writes words to fill in the blanks on a workbook page of details about the characters in a story.
In a simple log, a child draws and dates pictures to illustrate the differences that the child observes over time watching the egg of a silkworm develop into a monarch butterfly.	Using a provided page of illustrations depicting the cycle of a butterfly or moth, a child cuts out and pastes in sequence the pictures of the stages of that cycle.

Grading Open-Ended Products

When grading the work children produce, teachers want to insure that the grading is correct and fair. Compared to open-ended products, single-correct-answer tasks are simpler and more efficient to grade but at what cost? A major dilemma with single-correct-answer or fill-in-the-blank products is that children worry if their answers are correct so they look around at the responses of others or continually ask adults "Is this right?" A second concern is that children can complete the right answer for the wrong reason. For example, is the answer correct because the child understands the concept or skill, guesses well, eliminates sufficient alternatives to make a decision, or looks around for additional information? It is also probable that some children know much more than is assessed by the single-correct-answer task.

In school environments offering a wider array of learning experiences, teachers ponder how to grade open-ended products fairly. To begin, determine which evaluation criteria are most significant to the task. It is not difficult to grade criteria such as neatness and completeness and finishing on time; the conundrum is how to reflect the quality of the content information clearly. Quality involves both accuracy and complexity.

1. Grade the products for accuracy—products with correct responses score higher than products with errors.

2. Grade the products for the degree of complexity and depth expected for the grade level—more complex responses with in-depth information score higher than products with simple responses.

When appropriate, before children begin a task, show and discuss developmentally appropriate examples of some simple and more complex products that might result from the task. The demonstration enables children to envision different correct responses, leads them to understand that there are multiple ways to complete the task successfully, and increases their confidence that it is often appropriate to do something different from others. The examples are then put away to free children to proceed with their ideas. (When the examples remain on display, children may interpret that to mean that they should try to copy one of the responses.) Several examples follow of primary children's responses to open-ended tasks in reading, math, and science that illustrate the diverse levels of complexity children can exhibit when invited to participate in quality learning experiences in nurturing environments. The comparison challenges teachers to move beyond only encouraging a neat product appearance to encouraging different levels of responses that reflect children's uniqueness and continuous learning.

Example 4.2   Story Retelling

A boy loses a mitten. Animals get inside. There is not enough room. The boy gets the mitten back.

Example 4.3   Story Retelling

Nicki drops a mitten. Animals
find it and go inside to get
warm. It gets soooo full. Then
the bear sneezes and the
mitten flies back to Nicki. It's
funny that the mitten got so big.

These responses correctly retell a story that second-grade children read independently. The simpler response correctly uses words and uncomplicated drawings. The more complex response is also correct yet is more elaborated, includes an emotional response, and shares abstract thinking through the idea of a hotel. The child orally explains how the mitten is like a hotel because so many animals tried to live in it for a while.

Example 4.4   Ways to Make Nine

9

● ● ● ● ● ● ● ● ●

4 + 5 = 9
2 + 7 = 9
6 + 3 = 9
nine
1 + 8 = 9

Example 4.5 Ways to Make Nine

Nine   9   IX

/ / /   3 + 3 + 3 = 9
/ / /
/ / /   12 - 3 = 9

1   5 + 4 = 9

+ 8   7 + 2 = 9
___
9   20 - 10 - 1 = 9

These products result from first-grade children asked to use numerals, words, and illustrations to show all the ways they can think of to make nine. The simpler response has seven correct responses using sets and addition. The more complex response has ten correct responses using sets, both addition and subtraction, and incorporates multiple steps in two examples.

Example 4.6 Drawing an Insect Using an Initial

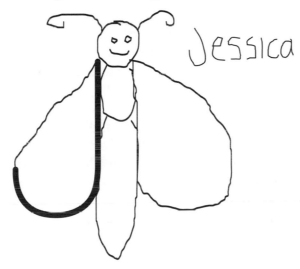

Example 4.7   Drawing an Insect Using an Initial

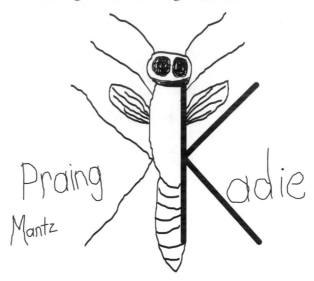

These illustrations were produced as a culminating product in a unit on insects. Kindergarten children were given a paper with the first initial of their name. The children were asked to use that letter to draw an insect and explain its attributes. The simpler response is correct and creates a complete insect but uses little detail. The complex response is more elaborate and purposefully incorporates several attributes of a praying mantis that the child orally explains such as three body parts, six legs, and *weak wings.*

A rubric is helpful when communicating evaluation decisions to children and families. A rubric lists the criteria and explains what is expected at each level of proficiency. Figure 4.3 shares an example of a rubric for open-ended products to illustrate how children with beginning reading and writing skills can benefit from rubrics that clarify degrees of success on a learning task. A further discussion and examples of rubrics for young children are provided in Chapter 5.

Figure 4.3 Rubric for an Open-Ended Product

Name _____   Date _____

Product _____   Points _____

Content 	Simple Limited understanding Points_____	Developed Correct Basic facts Points_____	Detailed Elaborates Interesting information Points_____
Capitals + Punctuation 	Mistakes Confusing Points_____	Mostly correct Uses . ? Points_____	Skillful Uses . , ? Points_____
Thinking 	Knows Points_____	Understands and explains Points_____	Analyzes Unique idea Points_____
Neat + Organized 	Not neat Hard to follow Points_____	Attractive Organized Points_____	Eye-catching Well organized Adds to content Points_____

Connecting Learning Experience

Evaluating an Open-Ended Product

Help young children learn that effort can result in higher achievement. Simulate the evaluation of a product appropriate to the developmental level of the class and engage kindergarten through third-grade children's high-level thinking by providing a poster of a rubric such as Figure 4.3 and product examples from children not in the class.

1. Show the class two examples of products representing very different levels of responses from a learning task familiar to the children. One of the products should be significantly less well done than the other product example. Children's experience with the task is important so they understand the intent of the assignment and know what was done to complete it.

2. Stress positive goals and effort rather than negative comments and elicit the children's reactions to each product by asking, "What is something done well? What else do you notice?"

3. Refer to one applicable criterion on the rubric poster and ask children to determine whether the stronger product earns the highest or lowest grade. Compliment them for thinking and seek clarification of their perspectives by responding, "You are really thinking about this. Why do you think that is so?"

4. Hold up the second product that is less well done and repeat the process for the same criterion. As children's interest allows, continue the evaluation discussion by referring to another criterion and comparing the products.

Initially, keep the process as concrete and brief as possible by focusing on two vastly different levels of products, discussing what was done well, and using only one criterion at a time for comparison. Share with the children the value of their effort. "It is my job to make sure that our learning activities are tasks you can do and that they will help you learn. It is your job to do all you can to help yourself learn."

Connecting Learning Experience

Extending Product Evaluation and Comparative Thinking

When children can successfully evaluate two examples of products demonstrating contrasting levels of achievement, extend their product evaluation and comparative thinking.

Extend children's development of self-assessment skills through continued class discussions and by actively involving the class or small group in assessing standards of quality.

1. Narrow the range of the differences in the proficiencies within the two compared products as children become more experienced with evaluation.

2. With experience, second- and third-grade children can consider three or more products that provide opportunities for them to discern levels of proficiency.

3. Have children use a rubric to model product evaluation with parents during child-involved conferences discussed in Chapter 6.

PORTFOLIO PRODUCTS

Portfolios should reflect the instructional climate and the individuality of the children. Rather than all portfolios containing precisely the same products, determine a menu of items to include in every portfolio for documentation of achievement, and whenever possible, children should select additional products according to their unique talents, interests, needs, and feelings of accomplishment. Ultimately, the intent is that the portfolio communicates the objectives of the learning environment and the capabilities and potential of the child.

The portfolio might exemplify only one content area such as a writing portfolio or encompass a cross section of the curriculum. In addition to curriculum priorities and school or district learning standards, products for prekindergarten through third grade must be developmentally appropriate to the children's learning profiles and expand beyond written paper and pencil tasks to reflect the many hands-on ways young children learn.

Figure 4.4, a chart of potential portfolio products, prompts ideas of the wide range of products appropriate for young children's portfolios. Teachers can review the examples to get ideas of potential products, consider explanations of what each is, and clarify purposes of what each can accomplish or of the value it can bring to a portfolio.

This chart is not inclusive of all of the kinds of work that could be selected and is not intended to dictate which products to include. Rather the list is a compilation of the products teachers verify as most helpful in providing assessment information for children, their families, and teachers. Skill sheets are usually not selected for portfolios, for example, because they feature more isolated skills and focus on correct versus incorrect rather than a child's potential and changes as a learner.

Review Figure 4.4 to consider any products that are developmentally appropriate to the class and match instructional priorities. Add other product categories that better reflect objectives. Some of the products are particularly effective when incorporated as learning log entries or repeated tasks—discussed as assessment techniques in Chapter 5.

Figure 4.4 Potential Portfolio Products

PRODUCT	EXPLANATION	PURPOSE
	What is it?	*What is its value in a portfolio?*
Art	Art pieces should include the child's natural, creative explorations and interpretations (rather than crafts).	Art reflects developmental levels, perspective, interests, graphic talents, abstract thinking, and creativity.
Audiotapes	A child tapes story retellings, math story problems, explanations of concepts, philosophical viewpoints, musical creations, problem solutions, ideas, oral reading, and reports.	Audiotapes verify vocabulary, fluency, creativity, high-order thinking, and concept depth.
Computer products	A child works at a computer to apply software, create word processing products, and complete other computer-generated products.	Computer-generated products indicate computer literacy, following direction skills, analysis, content-related academic skills, and applied concepts.
Cooperative investigation or group project	Products resulting from a cooperative learning task may be included in individual portfolios if the name of every group member is listed on the product. Furthermore, the product should be one that can be photocopied so more than one group member can select that product for their portfolios.	Cooperative products can reflect interests and encourage peer interactions. They can also verify emerging talents such as leadership, graphic design, or organization skills.

Dictations	An adult records a child's dictated explanation of a product or process. Prompt these dictations with statements such as *"Tell me about your work"* or *"Tell me how you did that."*	A dictation increases adults' understanding of the why and how of what a child does. It elicits the child's perspective and indicates vocabulary levels, sentence complexity, high-level thinking, fluency, and content depth.
Drawing and sketching information	A child can draw simple sketches to complete rebus writings, record a task, or represent observations and interpretations of data such as *"These two blocks make a square. I made a square!"*	Sketching allows a child to record information with less handwriting skill. It reflects developmental levels, fine motor control, interests, graphic talents, abstract thinking, and creativity.
Documentations of learning standards achievements	Specific products can be designated by a school or district to demonstrate a learning standard such as an assigned writing topic in third grade.	These products intend to provide a schoolwide assessment of one or more learning objectives.
Graphs, charts, or other graphic organizations of content	Some children produce graphic organizers to represent relationships and demonstrate the results of independent investigations. Graphic organizers designed by the child are particularly revealing of potential.	Graphic organizers promote interpretations, visual-spatial skills, and demonstrate specific skills or concepts applied in the task. Graphic tools provide opportunities for children to apply high-level thinking, data recording strategies, and organizational skills.
Interest inventory	Simple inventories can reveal children's interests so teachers can weave those interests into instruction.	Using children's interests helps teachers personalize learning opportunities and motivate children to want to engage in learning experiences.
Maps	Primary children can draw or use play dough or blocks to create simple maps to represent concrete experiences such as maps to their houses or maps of a room at home or school.	Map-making invites abstract thinking, symbols, perspective, size relationships, organization, and directionality skills.
Mathematical investigations	Math learning tasks should require children to use math skills and concepts to solve a problem beyond memorized math facts.	Original investigations can document problem solving, high-level thinking, and children's applications of math skills and concepts involving classification, number, seriation, spatial relationships, and temporal relationships.

Performance tasks	Performance tasks incorporate sets of skills across subject areas. They require students to perform or make products to demonstrate knowledge and skills.	These tasks involve hands-on, active learning applications in which students construct their own responses rather than select from presented alternatives. They invite children to integrate and transfer skills.
Photographs	Photographs are records of the child's math patterns, models, creative projects, dioramas, sculptures, constructions, experiments, or organizational systems. Embellish the information with a written explanation that accompanies the photograph. (Digital cameras are an asset for economy and almost instantaneous availability of the photograph.)	Photographs represent classroom scenes that depict the child's learning process and items that are too large to comfortably store in the portfolio. Photographs can highlight process, document group work, and represent three-dimensional products. They provide a record when no paper product is feasible.
Reading level	A child's reading level is verified by duplicating one or two examples of text that a child can read independently. Include the child's reflection of the text to demonstrate analysis skills.	Text samples authentically document reading level and a child's sophistication when interpreting written material. A list of books the child has read also documents reading level.
Repeated tasks	Repeated tasks are learning tasks demonstrating specific skills or concepts at different points of time.	This assessment device concretely substantiates how a child is changing as a learner.
Research and individual investigations	Research investigations are child-initiated learning experiences that pursue children's individual interests and enable them to find out what they want to know.	Research topics must be individually chosen, drive children to pursue information and develop expertise in one or more areas, and thus provide a valued means of responding to personal interests. The process challenges children to infer and reach personal conclusions. Research products reveal specific interests, synthesis, content depth, and the complexity level of a child's thinking.

Self-evaluations and reflections	Self-assessment requires that children reflect upon their learning experiences and products. Young children's reflections are guided with checklists and rubrics that invite children to mark what they did well or how well they learned.	Self-evaluations emphasize children's perceptions and the importance of their input. Children's work should reflect their voice and ownership.
Surveys	Surveys are a hands-on component of individual investigations, such as determining how many children in the class wear shoes that tie, slip on, or use Velcro™.	Constructing and completing surveys promotes children's interpretations, organization, visual-spatial applications, quantitative skills, oral language, and social interactions.
Tests or quizzes	A test or quiz presents a set of items that students complete or answer to evaluate their subject-matter knowledge and skills.	The intended use of a test or quiz is to objectively evaluate the child's level of mastery of tested skills and concepts.
Videotape	Videos document performances, a child's learning process, and oversized products. Limit videotape entries to three to five minutes to encourage the child to plan the presentation.	Videos present significant visual records and integration of skills and behaviors. They are an affective boost as children enjoy viewing themselves.
Written products	Original works written by a child are significant records of learning progress and development. Include stories, reports, scientific observations, poems, letters, and reflections.	Written products can demonstrate applications of content skills, vocabulary, high-order thinking, meaning construction, applications of written conventions, organization, concept depth, complexity, and handwriting development.

5

Techniques to Document Achievement

Assessment of young children is most valid in learning environments where children are actively engaged in authentic learning tasks. In these environments, teachers employ a variety of tools and techniques that assess the development of the whole child and that are customized to developmentally appropriate options. Effective and efficient methods of classroom assessment and evaluation of young learners include learning logs, repeated tasks, skill captions, analytical observation, checklists, and rubrics with simplified levels of reading and writing appropriate for younger learners. Select one or combinations of these techniques to incorporate in your assessment plan.

LEARNING LOGS

A learning log is a little book that children produce to demonstrate their skill levels of grade-level learning standards. Each page of the book lists a different skill for children to apply. When completed at the beginning, middle, and end of the year, these logs document the achievement of required learning standards as well as benefit the children, families, and teacher. Children benefit because they like the hands-on experience of producing little books and later enjoy reviewing the learning logs. Families enjoy seeing the books that increase their understanding and appreciation of their child's learning growth by comparing the skill levels over time. Teachers appreciate how each child can experience success working at her or his readiness level to complete each page. Simultaneously, however, teachers applaud how effectively the logs document the learning standards for which teachers are responsible.

Figures 5.1 and 5.2 are templates for the learning logs. On a folded copy of Figure 5.1, children write their names and the date to create the front and back cover when the book is stapled together. Children draw small illustrations on the cover to decorate and personalize their books.

Figure 5.1 Learning Log Cover

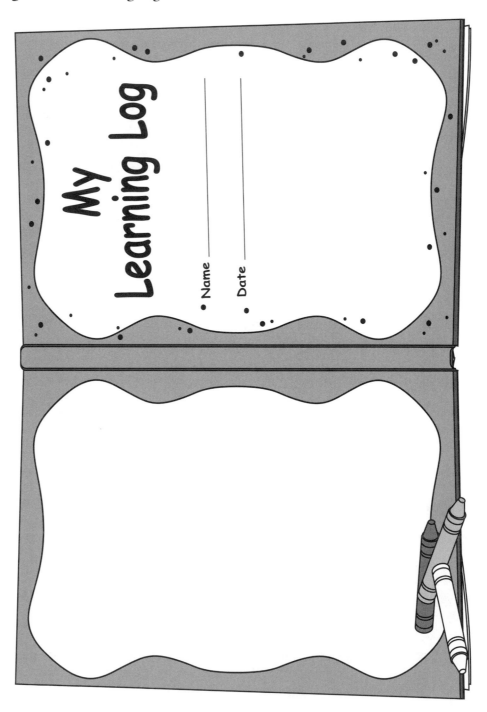

Figure 5.2 Learning Log Skills Page

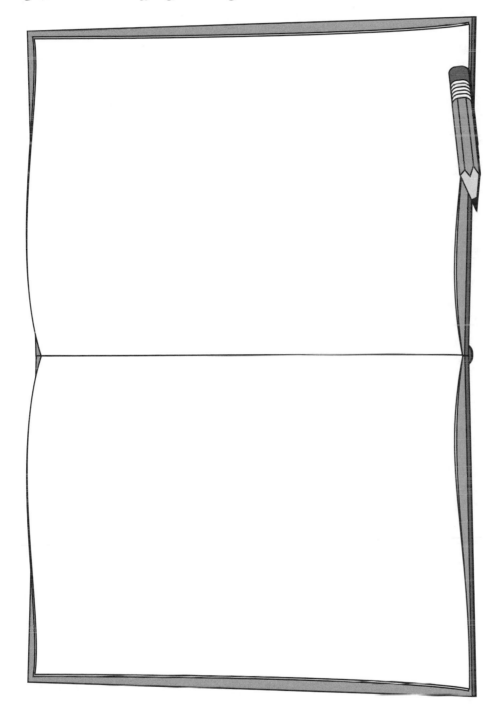

Teachers duplicate Figure 5.2 on the front and back of paper. This creates four pages for the learning log when the copy is folded in half. List on each copy a different skill for children to demonstrate. The skills reflect the learning standards in the curriculum and can incorporate different content areas. To determine which skills to include, review learning standards and focus on key skills children are to learn by the end of the year such as alphabet letters, words, numerals, math story problems, and geometric shapes. Typically, eight to twelve skills are included in a learning log.

Blank paper can be used for the learning logs but preprinting a skill on each page before children write conveys more information to parents and others who review the books. For example, when the books are completed the first time, a young child's writing may appear to be only scribbling unless a skill such as "I can write these letters" is preprinted on that page to clarify to others what skill the child is demonstrating.

Usually, children staple the skill pages in their books after they finish decorating the cover. Then they complete the learning logs by applying the skill designated on each page. Depending upon which is more appropriate to the readiness of the class, the entire book of skill examples can be completed at one setting or scheduled so children complete only one or two pages a day until the book is finished.

For additional assessment potential, some learning log pages include variations of the statement "I can read this." On those pages, the teacher duplicates content children are asked to read such as a random list of alphabet letters or numerals. As the child reads the items, the teacher circles the correct responses. Teachers can also attach a reading sample of a passage at a specific readability level that the child reads to the teacher to demonstrate fluency and reading level.

Many teachers predominately include the skills that focus on language arts and math since those content areas are so vital with prekindergarten through primary grade learners. Figure 5.3 lists some examples of skill statements to prompt teachers as they determine the significant skills they want to include.

Rather than limit the skills to language arts and math, any preferred content area skills can be demonstrated in the learning logs. The completed pages also include art applications as children draw pictures, sketch examples, or illustrate math problems. Some learning log pages such as "I can draw and write what I want to learn about in school" are useful to convey the interests of the children and enable teachers to integrate those interests into the class learning topics.

Children enjoy making and sharing these little books and typically look forward to repeating the task and then comparing changes between the beginning and later versions. Plan for children to complete one version of the book at the beginning of the year; then they complete a second and third version in the middle and again at the end of the year to document growth in skills and levels of achievements. These learning logs are particularly effective information to share with parents during conferences and at the end of the year.

Figure 5.3

Sample Skill Statements

Incorporate simple skills statements such as the following to guide students as they complete learning logs.

Language Arts
- I can draw me.
- I can draw my family.
- I can write my name.
- I can write these letters.
- I can read these letters.
- I can write these words.
- I can write this sentence.
- I can write a complex sentence.
- I can write a paragraph about _____. (Include a topic from science or social studies.)
- I can read this paragraph.
- I can write these opposites.
- I can write these rhyming words.
- I can write my address or phone number.
- I can draw and write about what I like to do inside.
- I can draw and write about what I like to do outside.
- I can draw and write what I want to learn about in school.
- _____
- _____
- _____

Math
- I can read these numbers.
- I can write these numerals.
- I can make this pattern.
- I can draw a set of _____.
- I can draw these shapes.
- I can name these coins.
- I can make a graph.
- I can write and illustrate a story problem that uses _____. (List one or more math operations or concepts.)
- I can write the steps to solve this problem.
- I can measure this _____. It's length is _____.
- _____
- _____
- _____

Learning logs are a special example of the assessment technique of repeating learning tasks to substantiate learning. Additional examples of repeated tasks are shared in the next section of this chapter.

REPEATED TASKS THAT EMPHASIZE SKILL DEVELOPMENT

Repeated tasks are learning experiences that children complete at one point in time and then later complete again to note gains in skills or achievements. This technique is an excellent assessment tool to demonstrate levels of achievement on specific learning standards over time. Pretests and posttests, a standard practice in classrooms, are actually examples of repeated tasks. Rather than limit this tool to testing, incorporate many other examples of authentic activities to use as repeated assessment tasks that accent skills and concept development.

As with learning logs, determine which skills to incorporate into repeated tasks by reviewing grade-level learning standards and selecting key skills children must demonstrate by the end of the year. Then plan and implement repeated tasks that incorporate those skills. Obviously, all repeated tasks are dated so informed comparisons of learning growth over time are possible.

Repeated tasks require that students complete a learning task the first time to provide benchmark information regarding their levels of readiness and learning needs. Background knowledge, beginning literacy, and fine motor coordination are particularly evident from these assessments with young children. These tasks are filed in the portfolio and then repeated one or more times later for comparative purposes. Analyze the results to document growth and determine continued learning needs and instructional pacing.

Many adults are unable to interpret skill levels appropriately when they view children's work. They only perceive how closely the children's skills approximate adult skills. Hence preschool and primary teachers need specific products in portfolios that concretely demonstrate students' growth or changes in skills and achievements. When tasks are repeated over time, the portfolio evolves to represent the changes in the child's learning accomplishments across the entire school year.

Whenever possible, maximize the potential assessment value of this technique by determining one or more specific repeated tasks for students to complete and file in their portfolios the first week of school. Asking young children to complete a self-portrait or a picture of their families is an effective first choice. Completing a picture of where they live is another appropriate initial item. The contrast of the results from the second, third, or more repetitions of the task throughout the year demonstrates the students' growth to the children, their families, and educators.

As a succinct way to verify to children how much they are learning, consider conducting three-minute celebrations. After completing a repeated task for the second or third time, declare that it is time for a three-minute celebration and invite each child to compare the results of two or more completions of that task. During this brief time, each child is encouraged to tell one other person what she or he notices and feels about comparisons of the products.

Many learning tasks can effectively be used as repeated tasks. Select those that most accurately reflect the instructional priorities and the required learning standards in your classroom. Self-portraits, family portraits, audiotapes, geometric shapes, picture interest inventories, and concept maps are some examples elaborated here. A short list of additional repeated tasks follows to prompt decisions about potential repeated tasks.

Self-Portrait

Each child draws a self-portrait. In classrooms with a wide range of readiness levels, these portraits run from scribbles to fairly refined human figures. When completed at the beginning, middle, and end of the year, this product illustrates the child's development of fine motor skills, self-image, and perspective. Asking children to add a sentence about the picture increases assessment potential by indicating the child's thinking level, feelings about self, vocabulary, and syntactic complexity. Scribe the child's ideas, or when appropriate, have children write their own sentence or more as a response to their portrait.

Family Portrait

Instead of or in addition to a self-portrait, each child illustrates a picture portraying the members of his or her family. These pictures indicate the children's awareness of their surrounding environment, size perspective, sequence, and knowledge of family member's individual identity. It also helps teachers understand more about each child's home environment and who they consider a member of their family, even when it includes a favorite pet. As with the self-portrait, asking children to add one or more dictated or child written sentences about the picture increases assessment potential by indicating the child's thinking level, vocabulary, and syntactic complexity.

Audiotape

Record an audiotape of each child retelling the same folktale or story at different times of the year. The resulting product is an effective oral language and comprehension device for both native language speakers and English language learners.

Individually, each child has a personal audiotape and records a retelling of a well-known folktale or story such as "The Three Little Pigs." This process takes only a couple of minutes for each child, and the product is an authentic measurement of story comprehension, sequence, and oral language development and fluency when the same story is recorded at the beginning and then again near the end of the year. Begin each entry on the tape by stating the date and the task: "Today is September 12, and T. J. is going to tell the story of 'The Three Little Pigs.'" Compare growth and refinement in vocabulary, sentence length, fluency, sequence, and syntactic complexity as a child retells the same tale later in the school year. The tape becomes a valued family present at the end of the year.

With primary children, the audiotape can also be used to record a reading sample documenting the child's independent reading level at multiple times during the year.

The reading samples can incorporate both fiction and nonfiction.

Geometric Shapes

The control required to draw geometric shapes incorporates the same fine motor skills and directionality that are needed to write letters and numerals. Provide large paper folded into boxes and ask children to draw a specific geometric shape in each box. Two to four boxes can be used with four- and five-year-olds. Four to six boxes on the paper are effective for the drawing task with six- to eight-year-olds. Dictate a different shape for children to draw in each of the boxes to measure fine motor skills, awareness of shapes, and readiness for writing between lines.

Drawing a straight line, an X, and a circle are complex enough to challenge four-year-olds. Adding a square, triangle, and a diamond are more complex and appropriate to challenge five- through seven-year-olds. Drawing the geometric shapes incorporated in the grade-level math curriculum make the challenge appropriate for second- and third-grade children. Asking children to number each box incorporates additional skills including number awareness, ability to reproduce numerals, and application of left to right and top to bottom directionality.

Picture Interest Inventory

Teachers want to understand children's interests and preferences so they can more effectively match instructional tasks to students' capabilities. Teachers also find that motivation to achieve increases when a child's interests are incorporated in learning experiences (Collins & Amabile, 1999). The problem, however, is that many inventory assessments are inappropriate for young children's skill levels. A picture interest inventory combines art with an investigation of a child's interests and is particularly an asset for spatial and visual learners who benefit from using art to communicate their ideas.

Fold large pieces of paper in half in order to create two drawing areas. On one half, ask students to draw pictures of their favorite things; on the second half, they illustrate what they are interested in learning at school. When more appropriate for specific children, write their dictation for each of their drawings. However, also encourage all of the children to write words and sentences about what they have drawn. Later review the inventories and incorporate that information into instructional planning. For example, consider expanding the animal unit to include skeleton structures and fossils if several children are interested in bones.

When completed at the beginning and then later in the year, this product illustrates the child's development of and progressive changes in fine motor skills, personal preferences, and interests. Adding words and sentences about the illustrations increases assessment potential by indicating the child's thinking level, feelings about self, literacy development, vocabulary, and syntactic complexity.

To vary the task for very young children or those with shorter attention spans, complete each half of the inventory at a different time. Simply fold the paper so only the half that children are to draw on is exposed. To vary the task for older children or those with more mature skills, fold the paper into four or even six boxes. Children then illustrate and write words or sentences about multiple things that are their favorites and that they are interested in learning more about at school.

Concept Maps

Concept maps are graphic organizers that illustrate topical information and relationships. As a repeated task, they are particularly effective when used as a pre- and postassessment tool. While they can be drawn in any number of ways, the simple format discussed here works well with young children. Concept maps are most applicable in first through third grades, yet some kindergarten teachers also report success using the technique with their classes.

Use Figure 5.4 or fold paper into four boxes in order to create areas on each sheet for different categories related to a current topic of study. On a sample copy or on the chalkboard, write the topic in the center and label a category in each of the boxes. Ask children to copy the title and category words on their map before they draw pictures and write words in each box to designate the information they know about that category. Have children complete a topic concept map as a topic of study begins and then later as a culminating task for that topic to assess their accuracy of information, depth, complexity, and understanding of the relationships within a topic. Completing the concept map as a repeated task enables children and families to compare how children's knowledge about the topic increases through their efforts and learning experiences.

Figure 5.4 Concept Map

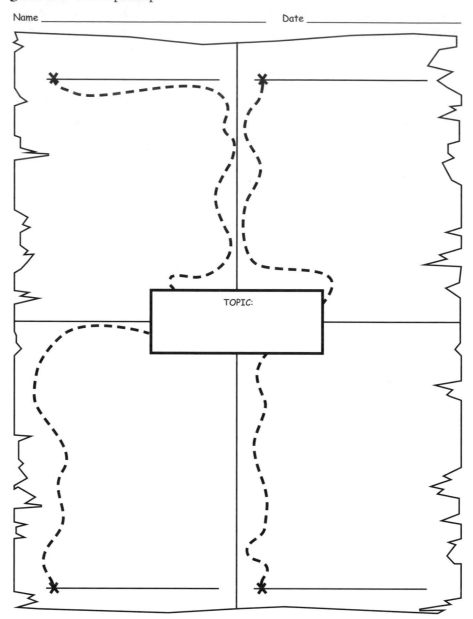

Figure 5.4 Concept Map

Example 5.4a Concept Map—Preassessment

Name _____   Date _____

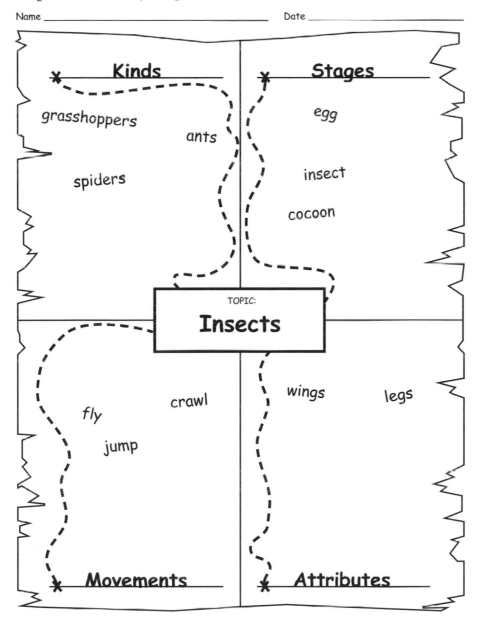

Example 5.4b Concept Map—Postassessment

Name _____   Date _____

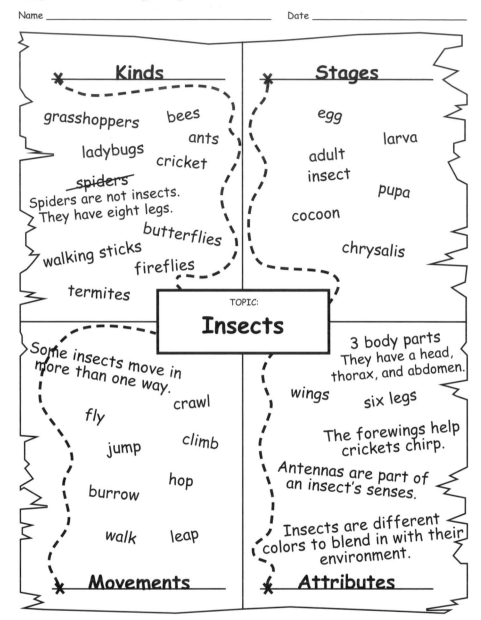

Additional Repeated Tasks

Each child

- produces a fine-motor sample by tracing one hand and cutting it out to paste on another paper;
- produces a handwriting sample that includes every letter of the alphabet (Figure 5.5 is one example of a brief response spaced for primary handwriting);
- writes and completes the hardest math story problem the child knows how to do that applies math operations and concepts currently being studied;

- writes the dictated high-frequency words to assess spelling mastery of the most commonly used words in reading and writing tasks;
- composes writing samples using narrative or expository writing;
- draws a map of where the child lives—the child is encouraged to include as many details and as much specific information as possible;
- writes the five most significant facts the child knows about a science, math, or social studies topic.

Figure 5.5 Handwriting

Name _____ Date _____

I can write this sentence using all of the letters of the alphabet.

The quick, brown fox jumps over the lazy dog.

SKILLS CAPTIONS

Family members may not clearly understand the instructional objectives and skills inherent in the products that young children complete. Skills captions are a device to use to compensate for this lack of understanding. A skills caption is a statement the teacher completes to photocopy and attach to each teacher-selected product in the portfolio. A skills caption explains the learning task and specifies the skills that are intended to be demonstrated when children complete the task. This technique enables parents to better understand the learning task and skills represented within that product. The captions also document that specific learning standards are woven into instruction as a natural component rather than an isolated skills activity.

Two variations of skills captions illustrate some of the possibilities for using this technique. Figure 5.6 is a skills caption on which the teacher explains a specific learning task and lists the skills imbedded within that task. The child's only input on this caption is to write his or her name on a copy of the caption before it is stapled to the product and filed in the portfolio. Figure 5.7 is a variation that increases the child's response. The teacher states the significance of the learning task, lists the embedded skills, and then duplicates the caption for each student. The child writes her or his name and adds a written response as a reflection on the bottom of the copy before stapling the copy to the product. Skills captions clarify the reason for the product being selected and clearly signal to family members and others who view the portfolio which items are teacher selected.

Figure 5.6 Skills Caption—Writing Skills

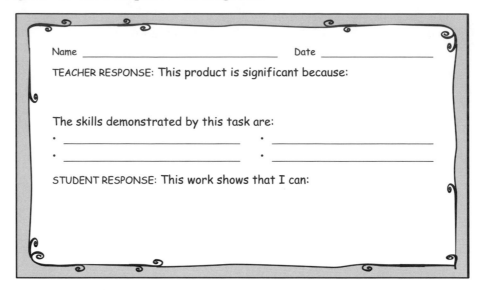

Example 5.6 Skills Caption—Writing Skills

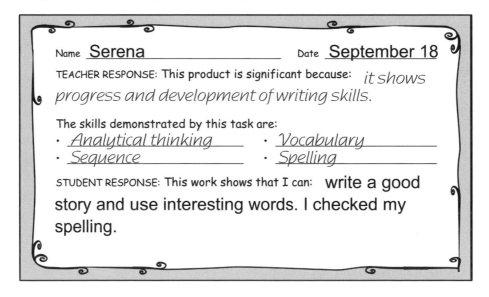

Figure 5.7 Skills Caption—Math Skills

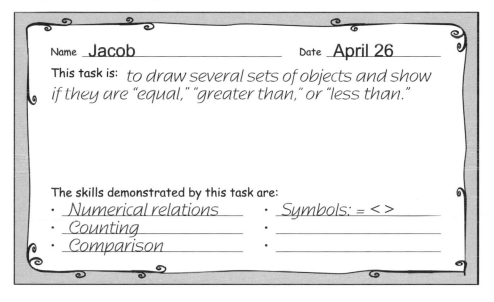

Name _____ Date _____

This task is:

The skills demonstrated by this task are:
- _____ - _____
- _____ - _____
- _____ - _____

Example 5.7 Skills Caption—Math Skills

Name **Jacob** _____ Date **April 26** _____

This task is: *to draw several sets of objects and show if they are "equal," "greater than," or "less than."*

The skills demonstrated by this task are:
- *Numerical relations* - *Symbols: = < >*
- *Counting* - _____
- *Comparison* - _____

ANALYTICAL OBSERVATION

Teachers who work with young children understand the importance of classroom observation. Since young children are more limited in their verbal ability to explain their learning and in their written ability to express themselves, teachers continually analyze children's behaviors to interpret what they see occurring in learning situations. In these classrooms, observation becomes a component of preassessment, continuing assessment, and culminating assessment. This valued preassessment tool guides teachers' decisions regarding the most appropriate instructional pace for specific children and at which levels to initiate instruction. As instruction progresses, observation is valued as part of the assessment of children's integration of skills and concepts and to determine continued instructional needs. At the culmination of a segment of learning, observation is one component in accumulating evidence of children's level of understanding.

The term *analytical observation* denotes that teachers do more than merely watch; they analyze as they observe to guide instructional decision making. As teachers analyze behaviors, they verbally interact with children to elicit the children's perceptions of learning. Talking with students about what they are doing provides a window to their thinking. Inquiry probes such as those in Figure 5.8 enable teachers to clarify information as children engage in learning situations. This metacognitive process parallels the procedure that teachers use when teaching children to reflect about their product selections for their portfolios.

Figure 5.8

Inquiry Probes

1. Tell me about the work you are doing.

2. What are you thinking about?

3. Tell me more about that.

4. What did you do to begin this work?

5. What do you plan to do next?

6. How did you figure that out?

7. Why do you think that is so?

8. What if this happened in a different order or sequence?

9. If this had not worked, what would you do?

10. How would you explain this to another child?

11. What changes could you make?

12. If needed, what would you do to get more information?

Values of Analytical Observation

Analytical observation

- helps define and refine teachers' interpretations of children's developmental levels, acquired proficiencies, learning needs, and the multiple facets of their talents and potential;
- clarifies awareness of special populations and learning capacities that standardized tests results may cloud;
- enables teachers to assess the process of learning as well as the products children produce;
- supports and integrates with other assessments and evaluations.

What Is the Focus of the Observations?

Teachers observe children's transfer and mastery of skills as well as their modality strengths and needs for instructional accommodations. Questions such as the following prompt the ongoing search for more productive information.

- *Skill integration.* Are children appropriately applying the specific skills they have been taught? How effectively are skills integrated into new learning situations and across content areas?
- *Skill mastery.* Which skills have specific children mastered? Which students require additional teaching, continued guided practice, or acceleration of instruction? Which learning experiences might better promote the needed practice? What flexible grouping adjustments are implied?
- *Modality preferences.* Which learning experiences do specific students most enjoy? Which learning experiences enable specific students to best succeed?
- *Instructional accommodations.* What flexible grouping implications might better accommodate these observed needs? What pacing adjustments might be beneficial? Is a child frequently demonstrating behaviors typical of children with learning differences or disabilities? What types of additional assessment information should be requested? What additional resources or accommodations are available to help these children experience continuous learning? Which children consistently demonstrate responses that exceed age-level expectations? What are their advanced areas? Which students would benefit from an accelerated pace and/or advanced level of instruction? What additional resources are available to enable these children to experience continuous learning?

Documenting Observations

Appropriately documenting analytical observations increases their validity and better enables other educators to understand what a teacher has come to know. A combination of assessment techniques is useful when documenting observations of children's processes and interactions.

- Document observations of children's processes as they work to complete learning tasks. Children's processes reveal attitudes and motivations as well as children's problem solving, depth of knowledge, skill integration, and level of achievement (documentation—checklists, lists of learning standards, anecdotal folder, and portfolios are effective).
- Document conversations among children as they work. Conversations provide insight into each child's prior knowledge, problem solving, vocabulary, level of achievement, interests, and social skills (documentation—anecdote folder, tape recordings, and checklists are effective).

Anecdotal Folder

An anecdotal folder is a tool that helps observation become more systematic and continual. A single folder is used to organize sticky-note anecdotes for all of the children in the class and encourage teachers to focus on each child at reoccurring intervals so quiet children do not slip through the cracks. The accumulated set of dated, specific anecdotes for each child guides instructional decisions and enhances the information shared at parent conferences and in report card narratives (Kingore, 2001).

Use a brightly colored folder so it is easily visible on a busy teacher's desk. Decorate the outside if desired, and use a marker to equally divide the inside into boxes—one for each child plus a couple of extra places for children arriving later in the year. The boxes need to be large enough for a sticky note to fit. Consider gluing a child's picture in each box and writing the name beneath the picture. This bonus makes the folder more attractive and is useful for substitutes and special program personnel trying to associate children's names and faces. Laminate the folder so it remains attractive and useful all year.

As an alternative, use a computer to create decorations for the cover, to organize dividing lines for the inside, and to add digital photographs of each child before printing on a file folder run through a printer. For large classes or to provide more writing space, overlap two folders with the right half of one glued to the left side of the other in order to make a trifold providing three eight-by-eleven-inch areas.

Once the anecdotal folder is prepared, place a blank sticky note in each box and write a child's name or initials with the date on each note. Set a reasonable goal to write continual records such as one anecdote for each child every three weeks. Then observe and record anecdotes of the children's learning behaviors. After a few days, notice which children do not have an anecdote recorded and strive to observe them particularly to avoid inadvertently missing a child. As your observation goal is reached, move the completed anecdotes to each child's folder and begin a new round of anecdote collections. Keep the notes in chronological order as you place them on the child's folder to increase their information potential.

Checklists

Checklists are an assessment technique with the potential to succinctly document learning and focus on important learning standards. While useful to both teachers and children, the caution is to avoid checklists composed of such an infinite list of isolated skills that the marking process is laborious and consumes extensive instructional time.

For teachers and other educators, brief checklists can guide assessment and provide a quick notation system to report children's progress and needs.

Figure 5.9 is an example of a template for such a checklist and is intended for multiple applications as a teacher focuses on different skills. Use one or more copies of the checklist to list the names of the children in one group. After entering one to three key skills on the form, jot down notes assessing skill applications while directing instruction with the small group. The same checklist might be used during several group sessions to note children's progress.

Figure 5.9 Small Group Checklist

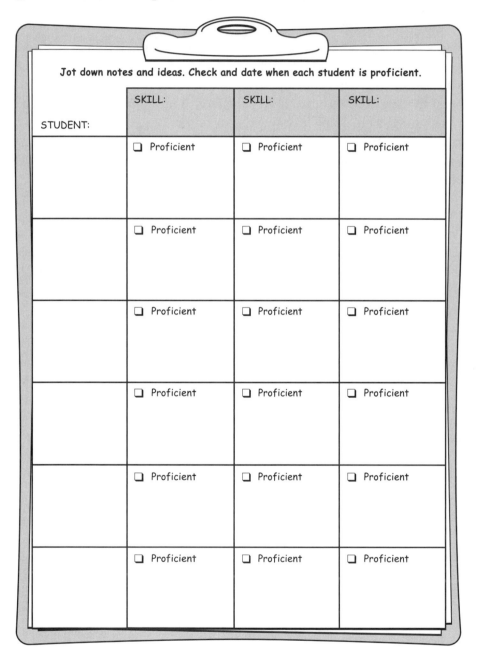

Primary children can use checklists to guide both their learning process and product development. As a process example, a simple checklist such as Figure 5.10 reminds children which skills to apply during a particular editing and revising session. The checklist is intended to help children focus on all of the parts of the task and check each item as they complete that part. A blank copy of the checklist, Figure 5.11, invites teachers to fill in different skills to use for another writing task.

Figure 5.10 Edit and Revise

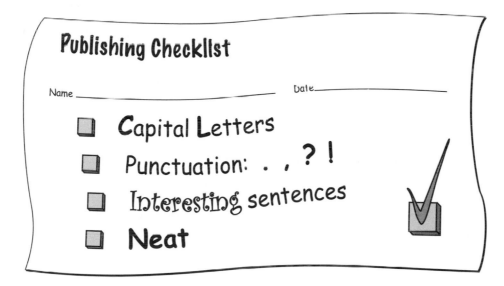

Figure 5.11 Edit and Revise

Checklists are also effective product guides that help children understand the requirements of completing a product. Figure 5.12, for example, guides a child through steps to create an original math story problem. A simple product checklist can keep children on track as they work and can allow them to share responsibility for their achievement. A product checklist can also be used for self-assessment to guide a child's reflection of the success of the work. Moreover, when attached to a product, a checklist increases the understanding of family members as they review the work.

Figure 5.12 Math Story Problem Checklist

Name _____ Date _____

Write an addition math story problem about your family. Complete the problem and draw its illustration. Check each item below when it is complete.

My story problem:
- ☐ Uses addition.
- ☐ Includes my family and me.
- ☐ Is written in complete sentences.
- ☐ Includes the number sentence.
- ☐ Has a total.
- ☐ Has an illustration.

Draw a picture of how you feel about your work.

While checklists are an effective and efficient assessment technique, they do not substitute for rubrics. A checklist is an inventory of the components of a task; rubrics specify the levels of proficiency to help children think more clearly about the characteristics of quality work. Tomlinson (2003) clarified that a checklist is not a rubric, as it does not guide thinking about quality; rather it is simply an inventory of requirements.

RUBRICS FOR YOUNG CHILDREN

Rubrics are an evaluation tool that communicates quality and grading guidelines. Preschool through primary-grade teachers might assume that rubrics are too complex for young children. Yet, young children obviously understand grading systems and quickly comprehend that a happy face, check plus (√+), or excellent is what they want to earn on their papers. Young children benefit when they view the specific information that a clearly constructed rubric offers so they understand how to succeed. The rubric for centers in Figure 5.13 is an example of a simple rubric beneficial for young children's self-assessment. After modeling and discussing with the whole class to explain and elaborate each level, children use the rubric to self-evaluate their level of success as learners and then draw on their papers the face they earned by their work during center time. The results could be combined into an evaluation for the grade book but often are intended to motivate higher learning behaviors and encourage children to examine and increase responsibility for their behaviors as learners.

Figure 5.13 Achieving at Centers

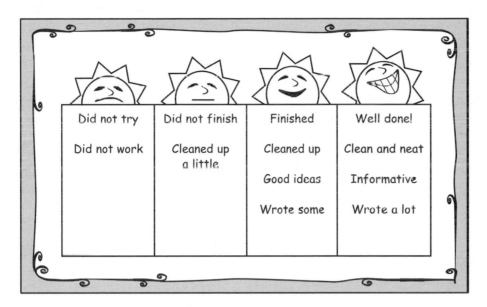

Did not try	Did not finish	Finished	Well done!
Did not work	Cleaned up a little	Cleaned up	Clean and neat
		Good ideas	Informative
		Wrote some	Wrote a lot

Connecting Learning Experience

Modeling the Use of Rubrics

As a class interactive activity, model how to use the achieving at centers rubric. Explain each level and invite children to role-play the different levels of responses. For example, a child might pick up one scrap of paper on the floor to represent *cleaned up a little*, and a second child might put away all of the used materials to represent *clean and neat*. Provide multiple opportunities for children to role-play different responses and participate in the range of learning behaviors represented on the rubric.

For variety if additional modeling is needed, an adult assumes the active modeling role and role-plays the lower end of the behaviors. To model *did not work*, for example, the adult pretends to mess around and has nothing completed on a paper. Children then model what to do differently each time such as acting out how to work on a written task and then holding up one of their written responses with words or sentences on it to show how much they wrote. Children enjoy the role reversal of being the ones who excel and teach the adult.

Rubrics are shared with children before they begin a learning task. The rubric is a guideline that clarifies the attributes of quality work and explains what each scoring level represents. As guidelines to quality, rubrics clarify to children and families what is expected in a learning experience and guide children to understand what they should do to reach higher levels of achievement. Rubrics are also grading guides that make evaluation more concrete and clearly understood by describing the requirements at each level of proficiency for each criterion in a learning task.

Children ably and accurately interpret rubrics constructed with fewer words and beginning readability levels that simplify the required reading. Pictures and rebus writing are another more concrete and simpler way to communicate quality to young children and English language learners.

The math rubric (Figure 5.14) is an example of a simple rubric for children and teachers to use to score achievement levels when completing a learning task. Provide copies of the math story problem checklist (Figure 5.12) and rubric (Figure 5.14) before children begin working. Children use the checklist to produce the product, and then children and the teacher use the rubric to evaluate the quality of the product. Fewer words and accompanying illustrations communicate the expectations of the math task, and they are easily used by children to self-evaluate the merits of their accomplishments. The criteria on the left communicate the important components of the task; the three levels of proficiency signal the degrees of success and help children know what to do to experience high achievement. After modeling, discussions, and guided applications as a class, primary children are able to use this rubric independently and accurately.

Figure 5.14 Math Rubric

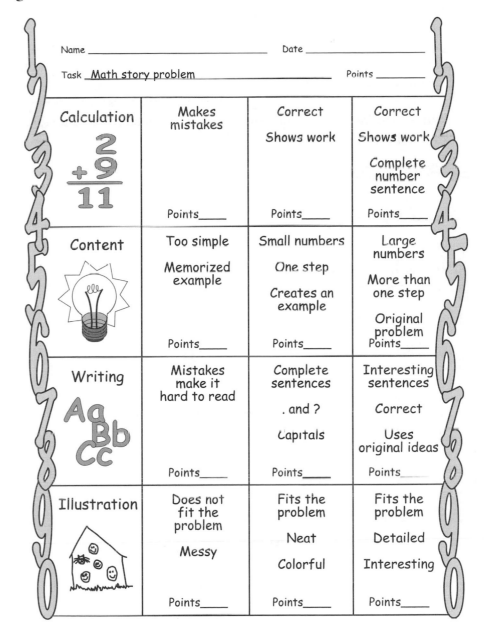

Strive to construct rubrics as generalizable as possible so a rubric has more than one application. The math rubric, for example, can be used for multiple tasks involving math story problems that incorporate different skills, operations, and topics. Different point values can be listed each time to designate the importance of each criterion and the total number of points for the task. For example, when a teacher wants to encourage more complex story problems, she might weigh *content* as ten points when the other criteria are each worth only five points. If desired, letter grades or holistic scores can be substituted for points.

To engage in self-evaluation, children complete the task and check each level they earned before handing the product to the teacher. When teachers want the task to result in a grade in the grade book, teachers can use a different color to evaluate on the same form.

Well-constructed rubrics provide children with a clear target and empower teachers with a standard by which to grade children's work more accurately and fairly. Use the checklist in Figure 5.15 to evaluate the effectiveness of rubrics you prepare or use with young children. Share rubrics with parents and other adults to more clearly communicate achievement standards and the specific skills and growth children accomplish.

Figure 5.15 Rubric Checklist

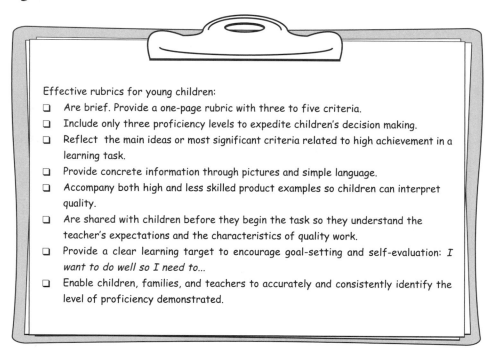

Effective rubrics for young children:
- ❑ Are brief. Provide a one-page rubric with three to five criteria.
- ❑ Include only three proficiency levels to expedite children's decision making.
- ❑ Reflect the main ideas or most significant criteria related to high achievement in a learning task.
- ❑ Provide concrete information through pictures and simple language.
- ❑ Accompany both high and less skilled product examples so children can interpret quality.
- ❑ Are shared with children before they begin the task so they understand the teacher's expectations and the characteristics of quality work.
- ❑ Provide a clear learning target to encourage goal-setting and self-evaluation: *I want to do well so I need to...*
- ❑ Enable children, families, and teachers to accurately and consistently identify the level of proficiency demonstrated.

TO GRADE OR NOT TO GRADE

There are occasions when teachers find it inappropriate to grade children's work such as when children are first engaged in learning a new skill. Teachers fear that grading initial attempts discourages effort and causes children to feel less confident or not want to risk trying something new. A problem develops, however, when parents want to see grades on everything to know the teacher's response. To resolve this conundrum, have a stamp made that states *draft* or *in progress.* Through communication at meetings or in letters, parents learn that these stamps mean that a product is only one step in a learning process and that evaluation will follow when appropriate at a later stage in the process. Children also use these stamps as they work on first drafts in writing.

6

Communication With Parents

Communication between home and school is more than just a nice thing to do. It is a significant component in the process of insuring that every child experiences continuous learning. We know that a substantial outreach to parents positively affects young children's learning (Commission on the Whole Child, 2007; High/Scope Educational Research Foundation, 2005) and that both teachers and parents benefit from exchanging knowledge about children (NAESP & CCG, 2005; NAEYC & NAECS/SDE, 2003).

Jones (2003) asserted that creating an educational partnership between school and home is crucial. In this reciprocal relationship, the more parents know about school objectives and procedures, the better they can support their children's learning. The more teachers know about the child outside of school, the better they can understand and guide the child's achievement of shared goals. The more children see their parents and teachers communicating the better they understand that learning is important and valued by those who care about children.

Portfolios are a particularly effective means of increasing productive communication among parents, a teacher, and a student through the concrete evidence the selected products provide. Many parents did not experience portfolios and authentic assessment procedures when they were in school. Educators help parents understand that this authentic assessment process provides a greater depth of information than report cards or standardized tests alone. For example in a parent conference, the child or the teacher shares specific products that support information and enable parents to gain a clearer understanding of their child's patterns of strengths, learning needs, interests, and progress than any report card can communicate. Viewing the actual work that children complete over time provides families a richer and authentic means of understanding what children are learning and what their depth of thinking is. After discussing a child's portfolio in a conference with the teacher, parents believe "You really understand my child," instead of "You like (or do not like) my child."

PARENTS COMMUNICATING WITH TEACHERS

Teach Us About Your Child

Schools need to seek information and goals actively from families who may otherwise feel reluctant to initiate communication. Parents often have information they would like to share with teachers yet worry if teachers would appreciate those details. Welcome parents to share their observations and participate in decisions about their children's education. Invite input by developing a form to guide parent's responses such as the communication form in Figure 6.1 and by inviting families to contribute information about the child. As an additional or alternative communication device, encourage parents to interview their child and share the child's perspective with the teacher by using Figure 6.2.

Figure 6.1 Teach Us About Your Child

In what ways do you feel we can best help your child at school?
Please share your experiences and observations to help us better
know your child. Continue writing on the back if you need more space.

Please return this to school by: _____

Child's name _____

Date _____

Your name _____

What do you most want us to understand about your child?

What should we know about your child's special needs?

How do you think your child feels about school?

What are your child's greatest interests or abilities?

Continued on next page.

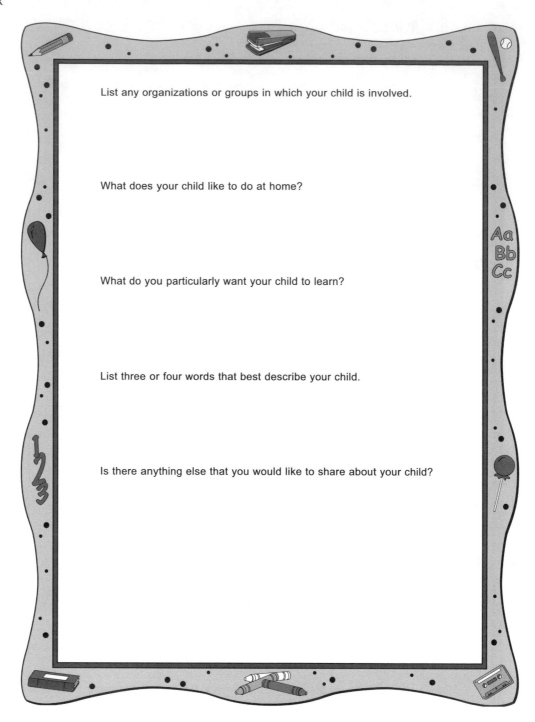

List any organizations or groups in which your child is involved.

What does your child like to do at home?

What do you particularly want your child to learn?

List three or four words that best describe your child.

Is there anything else that you would like to share about your child?

Figure 6.2 What I Want My Teacher to Know About Me

Interview your child and write down the information to share with the teacher.

Please return this to school by: _____

Child's name _____

Date _____

Your name _____

At school, I want to be called:

I am good at:

I am not good at:

I want to read or learn about:

One thing that would make school better for me is:

Notes to School

Offer simple forms to encourage parents to jot a note to the teacher. Parents certainly are not required to use those forms, but teachers find that some parents feel more comfortable and more encouraged to correspond when provided concrete initiatives such as note cards.

Figure 6.3 A Note From Home

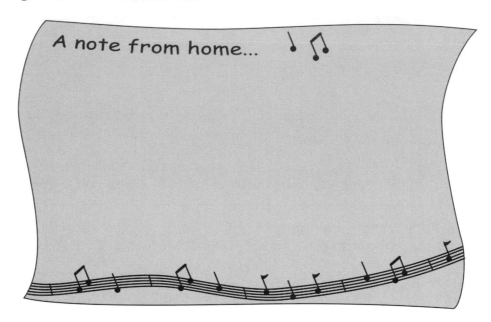

Figure 6.4 I've Been Thinking About...

PARENT-TEACHER CONFERENCES

This two-way, interactive conference is a collaborative communication forum between schools and families, which replaces the traditional approach that professionals know what is best and that parents need to be educated (NAEYC, 1997). Using authentically assessed information, the teacher shares concrete evidence of the child's progress and shows the family actual examples of that progress. Families can better understand the learning standards that schools are assessing and how the child is demonstrating the targeted skills and concepts.

In this partnership between teachers and parents, the teacher contributes information from the school setting and supports that data with observations and products from the child's portfolio. Parents are encouraged to participate, contribute insights from the home environment, and serve in a decision-making role to achieve the shared goals for their child.

Parent Preparation for the Conference

If not already used at an earlier time, parents can complete Figure 6.1, Teach Us About Your Child, to bring to the conference. They also prepare for the interactive communication by brainstorming insights about the child at home and writing questions to pose during the conference so they access needed information. The school can provide a sample set of questions or prompts such as the ones that follow for parents to consider before the conference:

- What does my child do at home that will help the teacher better understand my child's capabilities and potential?
- What does my child say about school?
- What is said about friends or other kids at school?
- How does my child act after school or in the morning just before going to school?
- I want to know how my child is doing in the following subjects or skills:

  _____

  _____

- Which subjects at school does my child like most?
- Tell me about my child's interactions with the other children.
- What are your goals for my child?

Child Preparation for the Conference

The child does not attend this conference. Therefore, to maintain ownership and responsibility in the portfolio products that represent the child's learning, the child selects the first item that the teacher will share with the parent at the conference. The child marks that product with a sticky note protruding from the product to mark its location clearly. When developmentally appropriate, the child also writes one or more sticky notes to attach to the product to explain what the child thinks about the work or wants the parent to notice.

Teacher Preparation for the Conference

In advance of the conference, select three portfolio products that demonstrate the main idea to share regarding the child's capabilities and potential. For example, select a product from the beginning, middle, and end of this learning segment to substantiate the child's growth in achievements or select three products typical of the special needs or behaviors that the student is demonstrating. During the conference, use this triplet of products to focus the interactive discussion. For example, a prekindergarten teacher selected three writing samples from the beginning four months of school to demonstrate how the child began writing isolated letters (*I A a*), used letters to represent a message beside a picture of a dinosaur (*I lk* "I like"), and then wrote more words and letters to complete sentences (*U R my frend!* and *I wnt a truk!*). During the conference with the parent, the teacher explained: "Adrian's work shows the development of his written skills over these four months. Notice how many more letters he is sounding out in his writing and how much more he wants to write to express his ideas. Let's talk about some of the things to watch for next in his writing."

To simplify management, place a sticky note protruding from the edge of each selected product in the portfolio. Some teachers like to number the sticky notes so the products are easily accessed in the preferred sequence. During the conference, turn to each product without taking it out of the portfolio.

Procedures for the Conference

Begin the conference by saying "Let's review the product your child selected for you to look at first." Share the child's selection and encourage reactions from the parents. Next encourage the parents to contribute insights from the home environment before proceeding to the three selected products that demonstrate the main point the teacher wants to demonstrate during the conference. Invite the parents to respond to those products with their perceptions and share any questions or concerns. Also discuss targeted learning objectives and standards for the upcoming learning period so parents gain a perspective of their child's continued learning developments and can serve in a decision-making role to achieve shared goals for their child.

It is important for parents to understand that the portfolio will be reviewed more often than just during a parent-teacher conference. As the conference concludes, make certain that parents are aware of other scheduled times when children can share their portfolios with their family such as when the portfolio is brought home to share overnight, on a parent night at school, during a child-involved conference, or at the end of the year when the portfolio is bound and presented to the family to keep.

CHILDREN COMMUNICATING WITH PARENTS

Products Taken Home

Children regularly take home any products not selected for the portfolio. Before a product is taken home, guide potential home conversations about schoolwork by having children briefly reflect and prioritize how their work will be viewed at home. On one product, children mark their favorite item or something they did well, and then place that product on top so it is considered first when sharing schoolwork at home. For example, a kindergarten teacher had her children use a star to mark one such item on a product before they left for the day. In this way, family discussions with the children more readily focus on the child's perceptions rather than only the grade. The teacher knew her system was a success when a parent sent this note about her kindergartner.

Example 6.3 Parent Note

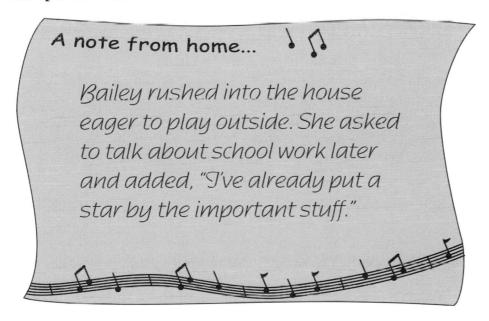

Other teachers invite children to use colored highlighters or sticky notes to mark products with their reflections or responses. The objective of this school and home communication is to help children and parents focus on what is being learned rather than only the grade on a paper.

Using the Portfolio

Sharing Portfolios During Child-Involved Conferences

Child-involved conferences, sometimes referred to as student-led conferences, provide a significant opportunity for children to use the portfolio to communicate their achievements, interests, and potential to their families. Portfolios increase the effectiveness of these communications because the products provide parents with directly observable and understandable evidence concerning their child's performance.

Schedule one or more times during the school year when children lead a conference at school with their parent or family representative. These conferences evolve from the need to accent the child's ownership and responsibility in learning. The format elicits the child's perceptions of learning rather than the practices of the past where conferences occurred to talk about the child but the child had no responsibility or input of information for the conference.

Children benefit from these conferences when the interaction

- showcases what they have produced and accomplished;
- requires children to plan, organize, and orally present information;
- accents the children's active role in assessment;
- provides an authentic audience for their work.

Parents benefit from these conferences when the interaction

- is led by the child and not dominated by an adult;
- invites parents to listen and discuss with the child what the child is learning and has achieved;
- enables parents to understand the child's perspectives of learning experiences;
- encourages parents to participate in setting learning goals with their child.

Child-involved conferences typically take one of the following two forms:

1. In one type of child-involved conferencing, multiple child-parent conferences occur simultaneously at school while the teacher facilitates the overall process. This conference focuses on child-parent interaction and communication.

2. A second type of child-involved conferencing is a three-way conference where the child, parent, and teacher all participate. In this conference format, only one conference occurs at a time, and the focus is the communication among the three people most vested in the child's learning.

Few prekindergarten classes attempt child-involved conferencing. In kindergarten through third grade, however, teachers report that children successfully complete these conferences and enjoy the process when the conferences are clearly organized, the children are well prepared, and the experience is developmentally appropriate and concrete as children incorporate learning opportunities throughout the entire room. Specifically, children use the room and all of its contents as concrete prompts for their thinking and explanations to family members. Rather than limit interactions to a typical sit-down conference or show-and-tell, teach children how to move purposefully about the classroom to convey information and experiences. Children know quite a lot about their learning environment and more freely share information when they move about the room.

Kindergartners *walk* around the room with their parent or family representative to explain class centers and activities; children in first through third grades *read* around the room by reading most of the print posted in the room to demonstrate reading skills to a parent or family representative and explain the learning experiences in the different locations. With their families, kindergarten through third grade children then sit at their table or desk to view and discuss selected items in their portfolios. The emphasis is on the child's active role in the learning environment rather than the decorations in the room.

Preparing Children for Child-Involved Conferences

Product selection. With facilitation, children plan three items to share during the conference. Teachers usually select a fourth item that each child shares as a benchmark piece. Ensure that a skill caption form is attached to that fourth product so parents know that item is required. Limiting the number of items requires children to think and plan in advance what to share. A small number of items also serve to control the time needed to complete the conference. Children flag each selected product with a sticky note so each is easily found when sharing with a parent.

Practice. A product show-and-tell is an effective rehearsal for children learning to discuss their work with someone. Children select one item from their portfolio, plan what they want to say about it, and then sit in pairs to share that item with another child. This procedure can be repeated as needed to increase children's comfort levels and practice talking about their work.

During practice sessions, children are guided to explain different factors such as any of the following that a parent might want to ask during the conference.

- *Time.* When did you do this? How much time did it take?
- *Feelings.* How do you feel about the item? What is your favorite part?
- *Purpose.* Why is this work in your portfolio? What does it show?
- *Quality.* What is something you did well? What is something that was hard to do?

Role-play. Research demonstrates that sociodramatic play is an important learning tool for young children (Bergen, 2002; Levy, Wolfgang, & Koorland, 1992). To become more comfortable and learn communication procedures, children can role-play discussing a product with someone else who pretends to be the parent. Initially, either the teacher and a child or two teachers role-play a child-involved conference in front of the class to model what the conference looks and sounds like. Then children work in pairs with one child role-playing the parent while the other child discusses a portfolio product. Later, the two children switch roles and play again. The pair concludes the role-play by thanking each other for participating. Children are surprisingly perceptive when playing the role of the parent.

Procedures. During the child-involved conference, the child and family representative sit side by side to better view and discuss the selected products. At the end of the conference, the child thanks the family representative for coming to the conference. After the conference, the teacher offers family members a letter template or blank paper and invites them to write a letter to their child about the conference.

Figure 6.5 Child-Involved Conference Response Letter

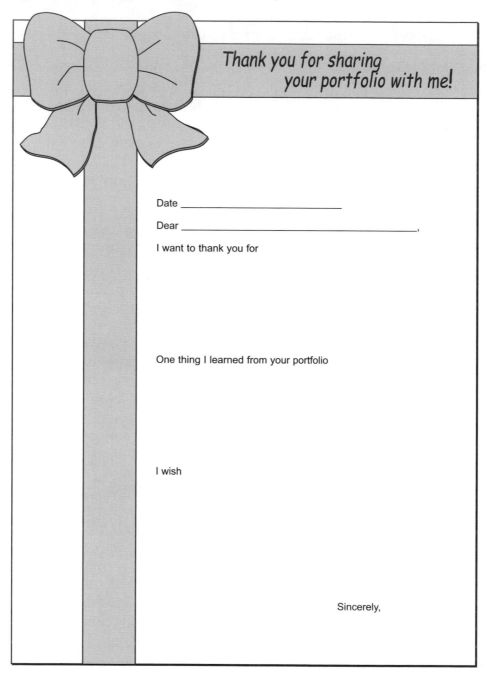

Sharing Portfolios at Parent Nights and Portfolio Exhibitions

Portfolios are major communication tools when, for example, it is back-to-school night or teachers are meeting with parents during American Education Week. Some schools plan additional schoolwide portfolio occasions for parents. Referred to as portfolio exhibitions, the classes cooperatively plan this special opportunity and invite the parents to participate. This alternative works well during lunchtime or combined with school events such as curriculum night. As with child-involved conferences, children use the room and all of its contents as concrete prompts to share and explain to family members in addition to discussing portfolios.

Figure 6.6 Invitation to a Portfolio Exhibition

Date _____

Dear Families,

You are invited to a portfolio exhibition at school. Please come to our class on_____ at _____. Your child has prepared a portfolio of valued accomplishments and would like to spend about 15 minutes showing you how much is being learned.

Sincerely,

Connecting Learning Experience

Preparing for a Parent Night or Portfolio Exhibition

The class can work together or in cooperative committees to prepare for this special occasion. As a class, brainstorm and list what needs to be done. Then divide the tasks and form committees so all of the children are involved in respectful tasks. Some examples of tasks for groups of children include preparing simple refreshments, counting and arranging cups and napkins, creating a welcome sign, designing a bulletin board, and organizing classroom space.

Sharing Portfolios at Home

Invite children to review and discuss portfolios with their parents at home. At designated times, children take their portfolios home overnight and return them the next day. This is particularly valuable for parents who work outside the home and may be less available during school hours. Portfolios can be taken home for review when the home environment allows the portfolio to be safe and respected overnight. In specific cases where a teacher deems that a portfolio will not be protected at home, copies of the work can be sent in place of the originals.

A few days prior to sending the portfolios home, send an invitation such as Figure 6.7 to the families about the children sharing their portfolios at home. Advanced notice encourages parents to set aside time to be involved with their child.

Figure 6.7 Sharing the Portfolio at Home

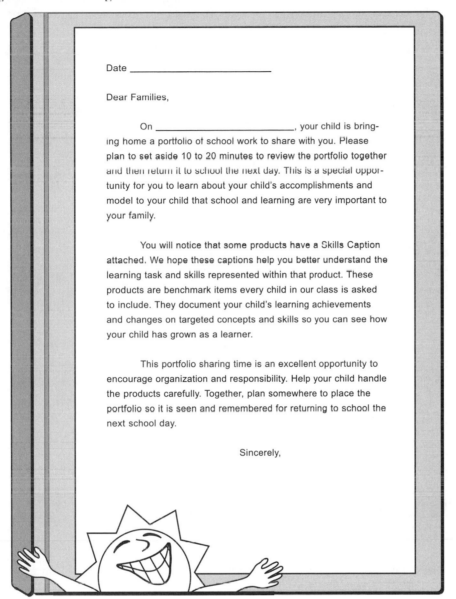

Date _____

Dear Families,

On _____, your child is bringing home a portfolio of school work to share with you. Please plan to set aside 10 to 20 minutes to review the portfolio together and then return it to school the next day. This is a special opportunity for you to learn about your child's accomplishments and model to your child that school and learning are very important to your family.

You will notice that some products have a Skills Caption attached. We hope these captions help you better understand the learning task and skills represented within that product. These products are benchmark items every child in our class is asked to include. They document your child's learning achievements and changes on targeted concepts and skills so you can see how your child has grown as a learner.

This portfolio sharing time is an excellent opportunity to encourage organization and responsibility. Help your child handle the products carefully. Together, plan somewhere to place the portfolio so it is seen and remembered for returning to school the next school day.

Sincerely,

Connecting Learning Experience

Composing an Invitation to Parents

As an authentic language arts activity, work together as a class to compose a letter to inform parents about their opportunity to review the portfolios at home. With very young children, discuss the occasion and brainstorm the kinds of information the parents need to know. Facilitate as the children determine what information needs to be written at the beginning, the middle, and the end of the invitation. Then scribe the invitation as the children participate. Duplicate a copy of the invitation for each child to write the date and name on the copy. If room or interest allows, include a place for a pattern or illustration by the child to personalize the invitation further.

With first- through third-grade children, brainstorm together and scribe a word bank of related words. Orally plan information and possible sentences for the beginning, middle, and end of the invitation. Then each child composes an original invitation to family members. If desired, provide copies of one of the border templates in the Appendix for the children to use as the stationery for their invitation.

Sharing Portfolio Books at the End of the Year

Another opportunity to share the portfolios is extended when the portfolio is bound and taken home at the end of the school year. Prepare a note that reminds families that these published portfolio books are very important to children and invites family members to plan to celebrate the book with the child when it arrives at home. A sample note is provided at the end of the next chapter as one component in the process of finalizing the portfolios at the end of the school year (i.e., Figure 7.8 Family Letter: Portfolio Books).

TEACHERS COMMUNICATING WITH PARENTS

Parents look to teachers for information and welcome ideas for nurturing learning at home. Parent-teacher conferences are one forum schools use to communicate with families. Additionally, share information about assessment with parents through school visits, meetings, a curriculum calendar, and letters.

Invite Parents to School

Encourage parents to spend the day with their child at school to emphasize the importance of parental involvement. Parents not available for an entire day can elect to eat lunch at school with their child.

Parent Meeting

Plan a meeting with parents to discuss assessment and learning objectives. Review the following suggestions to prompt decisions regarding the information to incorporate in the meeting. Expand the list with additional ideas to address specifically the needs of children.

Parent Meeting Agenda

- Recommend that parents talk with their children about work at school and elicit their children's perceptions of learning experiences.
- Explain authentic assessment and discuss the educational benefits it provides in the classroom. Invite parents to recall and contrast assessment and evaluation procedures when they were in school.
- Provide an overview of assessment plans and include specific information about the children's involvement and responsibilities.
- Model the portfolio process as it will be used so the adults can benefit from seeing concrete examples.
- Use an overhead transparency of a child's repeated tasks from the beginning, middle, and end of a previous year to demonstrate to parents how clearly products can document growth and level of achievement.
- Share a videotape of a child-involved conference from a previous year or have a former student work with you to role-play a portfolio conference.
- Discuss the multiple opportunities parents will have to review children's portfolios and discuss what has been learned.
- Briefly explain what will happen to their child's portfolio at the end of the year.
- Elicit parents' perspectives and reactions to the content of the meeting.
- Establish an open-ended invitation for two-way communication between parents and teachers.

Curriculum Calendar

Create a monthly curriculum calendar listing the key topics and points of interest included in class learning experiences for the month. The calendar provides a brief curriculum overview so families have a general view of the sequence of the curriculum as well as a sample of the skills and concepts of current study. This communication device provides concrete information to guide parents' interactions with their children after school. Parents learn to avoid asking the generic question "What did you learn at school today?" Instead, parents discover that children are more engaged when prompted with a specific reference to a curriculum item listed on the calendar for that day such as "Tell me what the class was doing with the chicken bones." The calendar helps parents talk with their child and ask about a specific item scheduled for the day.

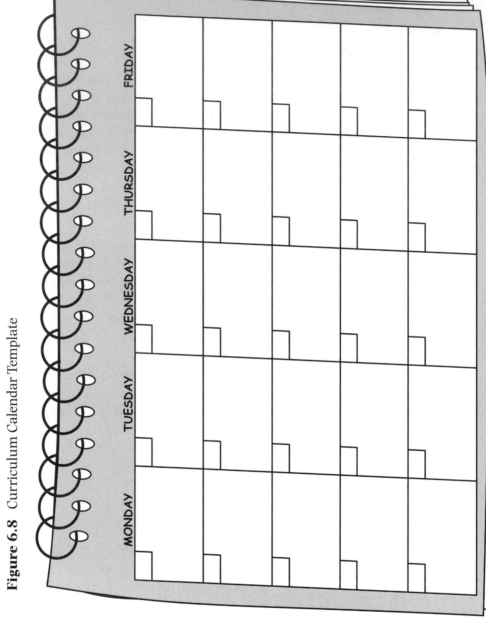

Figure 6.8 Curriculum Calendar Template

Example 6.8   Curriculum Calendar Partial Example

Letters to Families

Periodically, send informative letters to families to increase their understanding of portfolios, of authentic assessment procedures, and of how they can actively support their child's learning. Letters are effective communication tools to inform parents about learning objectives and increase the likelihood that they will understand and support the process.

"What you're not up on, you're down on" (Dutch adage).

Plan several letters to use at different times throughout the year. A set of sample letters is shared here to represent the content other teachers and parents considered helpful. These letters are intended as examples of potential content and are not presented in a recommended sequence for copying and sending home. Busy teachers more quickly produce the informative letters they need when provided with sample letters to consider and revise. Adapt these letters and create original informative letters incorporating simple visual appeal such as the stationery templates in the Appendix.

Overview of Parent Letters

Introducing the portfolio process. Figure 6.9 is most effectively used when beginning portfolios. The objective is to help parents appreciate how the portfolio products help them learn about their child.

Talking with your child about school work. Figure 6.10 accents the value of talking with children about schoolwork to support the child's learning. This letter also addresses the problem of schoolwork completed by someone other than the child alone.

Integrating high-level thinking. The letter in Figure 6.11 accents the value of the analytical process involved in selecting items for the portfolios. Sharing specific criteria that children use as they select an item helps parents understand that portfolios are more than collections of children's best work.

Encouraging responsibility. Use Figure 6.12 as a vehicle to discuss the importance of children being responsible citizens and to share ways that families can encourage responsibility at home.

Participating in child-involved conferences. Use Figure 6.13 to help parents understand their role in a child-involved conference. This information prepares family members to interact more effectively and positively with the child as the child shares the work selected from the portfolio. Posing specific questions to ask during the sharing process helps parents maintain a positive experience with the child.

Supporting learning at home. Figure 6.14 acknowledges the important role that home environments play in a child's learning and offers suggestions for how family members can support learning.

Understanding and supporting learning standards. In response to current news stories and headlines about education, parents are often interested in how national, state, and area learning standards affect their child's achievement. Figure 6.15 helps parents understand how to support the school's learning objectives for their children.

Figure 6.9 Introducing the Portfolio Process

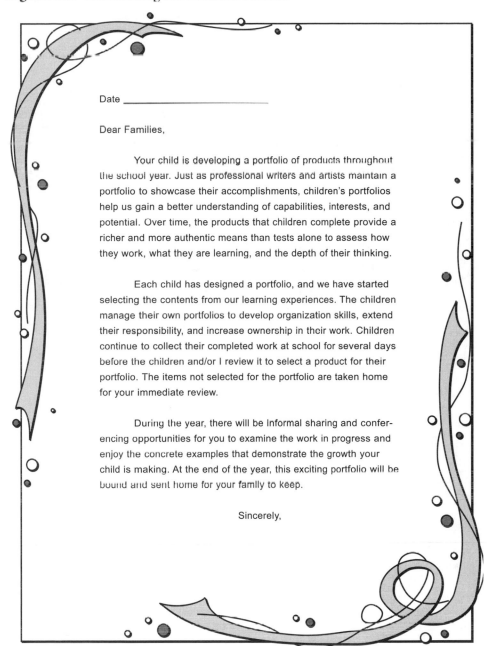

Date _____

Dear Families,

Your child is developing a portfolio of products throughout the school year. Just as professional writers and artists maintain a portfolio to showcase their accomplishments, children's portfolios help us gain a better understanding of capabilities, interests, and potential. Over time, the products that children complete provide a richer and more authentic means than tests alone to assess how they work, what they are learning, and the depth of their thinking.

Each child has designed a portfolio, and we have started selecting the contents from our learning experiences. The children manage their own portfolios to develop organization skills, extend their responsibility, and increase ownership in their work. Children continue to collect their completed work at school for several days before the children and/or I review it to select a product for their portfolio. The items not selected for the portfolio are taken home for your immediate review.

During the year, there will be informal sharing and conferencing opportunities for you to examine the work in progress and enjoy the concrete examples that demonstrate the growth your child is making. At the end of the year, this exciting portfolio will be bound and sent home for your family to keep.

Sincerely,

Figure 6.10 Talking With Your Child About School Work

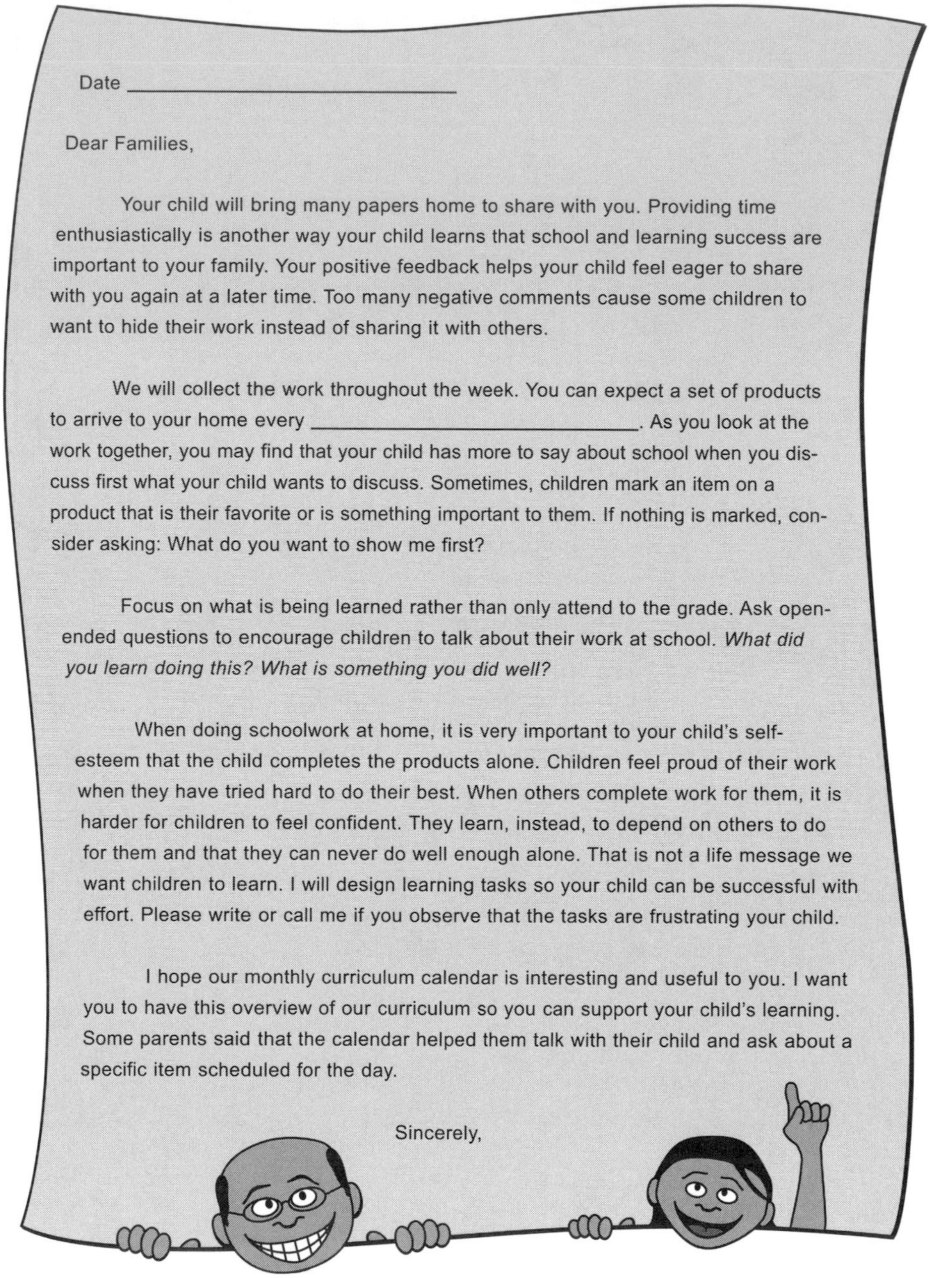

Date _____

Dear Families,

    Your child will bring many papers home to share with you. Providing time enthusiastically is another way your child learns that school and learning success are important to your family. Your positive feedback helps your child feel eager to share with you again at a later time. Too many negative comments cause some children to want to hide their work instead of sharing it with others.

    We will collect the work throughout the week. You can expect a set of products to arrive to your home every _____. As you look at the work together, you may find that your child has more to say about school when you discuss first what your child wants to discuss. Sometimes, children mark an item on a product that is their favorite or is something important to them. If nothing is marked, consider asking: What do you want to show me first?

    Focus on what is being learned rather than only attend to the grade. Ask open-ended questions to encourage children to talk about their work at school. *What did you learn doing this? What is something you did well?*

    When doing schoolwork at home, it is very important to your child's self-esteem that the child completes the products alone. Children feel proud of their work when they have tried hard to do their best. When others complete work for them, it is harder for children to feel confident. They learn, instead, to depend on others to do for them and that they can never do well enough alone. That is not a life message we want children to learn. I will design learning tasks so your child can be successful with effort. Please write or call me if you observe that the tasks are frustrating your child.

    I hope our monthly curriculum calendar is interesting and useful to you. I want you to have this overview of our curriculum so you can support your child's learning. Some parents said that the calendar helped them talk with their child and ask about a specific item scheduled for the day.

                          Sincerely,

Figure 6.11 Integrating High-Level Thinking

Date _____

Dear Families,

Portfolios integrate high-level thinking skills. Your child is demonstrating high-level thinking and decision-making skills each time we select a product for the portfolio. As we work together to select a product, children are assessing, increasing their awareness of quality, and making judgments.

As children help determine which products to include, they learn to think about important evaluation criteria such as:

- *What am I learning to do?*
- *What can I do now that was hard for me earlier?*
- *What do I like to learn?*
- *What is important to me?*
- *What examples should I keep in my portfolio to represent my learning growth throughout the year?*

Judging the merits of work is a life skill your child is practicing through the portfolio process. Children frequently look to adults to tell them about the quality of some work by asking: Is this good? Do you like it? When a child asks if we like a product, we try to respond: Do you like it? What you think is very important to me.

Please contact me at school if you have questions or information to share about integrating high-level thinking in our learning environments at home and school.

Sincerely,

Figure 6.12 Encouraging Responsibility

Date _____

Dear Families,

One value of the portfolio process we do at school is that it helps children learn to organize and manage their work. As children learn the benefits of order, they begin to view themselves as capable. There are several ideas that families can use as tools to model at home and help encourage children's responsibility.

1. Organize papers brought home from school. Have children assist in the decision making about what to do with school products.
   Which ones do you want to place on the refrigerator?
   What should we take down now to make room?

2. Designate a highly visible location at home to place anything that is returning to school, such as notes or school supplies. Seeing these things before leaving for school prompts children to remember them.

3. When possible, set up a small location at home to organize books to read and have children return a book to its place after a story is shared.

4. Together, label places for toys and objects in your child's bedroom to organize and model the adage: *A place for everything and everything in its place.*

Here are some additional suggestions for responsibilities many young children can assume at home to let them know that they are making a contribution to their family.

- Get the mail.
- Mark off the grocery list as items are located when grocery shopping.
- Help put some groceries away in designated places.
- Follow a schedule for feeding or caring for a pet.
- Help make the bed.
- Have a place in the yard or garden to care for.
- Prepare a simple food item.
- Count out needed items and set the table.
- Clean up what they spill or drop when eating.

Please send a note with other ideas that work well in your family. We can collect them and share with each other in another letter.

Sincerely,

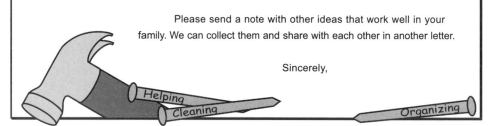

Figure 6.13 Participating in Child-Involved Conferences

Date _____

Dear Families,

Your child has selected three products to share with you at our special child-involved conference. In addition, I selected the product with the skill caption attached and asked your child to discuss it with you. As you review the work together, please remember that your child has worked very hard and is eager to show you how much has been learned and accomplished since the beginning of this school year.

The following suggestions help to ensure a positive experience for your child.

1. Your child will walk with you around the room to tell you about our learning environment. Encourage your child to talk more than you. Careful listening helps you understand your child's accomplishments and feelings.

2. When you sit together to review the portfolio, let your child lead. Ask: What do you want to show me first? You can probe for more information by adding: Tell me some more so I understand.

3. Continue asking questions that let your child explain the products and learning process. Your child has practiced responding to open-ended questions such as:
   - *When did you do this? How much time did it take?*
   - *How do you feel about the item? What is your favorite part?*
   - *Why is this work in your portfolio? What does it show?*
   - *What is something you did well? What is something that was hard to do?*

4. Comment positively on the strengths and improvements in your child's work. Encouragement helps your child know you are proud of what is learned.

We can learn so much from your child's perceptions of learning. If you have questions, concerns, or insights about anything you see or hear, please contact me at school so we can discuss them together. Thank you for participating in your child's education.

Sincerely,

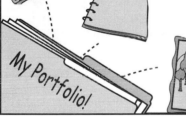

Figure 6.14 Supporting Learning at Home

Date _____

Dear Families,

Some of you have asked what you can do at home to help support your child's learning. Here is a list of possibilities to get you thinking of what is most effective for your family.

- Model reading and writing at home by personally engaging in authentic reading and writing tasks, such as reading books or newspapers and writing notes to your child.
- Seek ways to use math experiences at home, such as counting or measurement tasks, playing math-related games, and using math software. Develop shopping lists that involve purchasing different quantities of items. Check the weather chart in the newspaper to determine temperatures and plan clothing for the next day.
- Model the importance of reading by scheduling a time devoted to reading every day.
- Talk with your child as you read a story together. Elicit your child's reactions by using open-ended questions such as: What do you think he will do next? Why did that happen? Vary the interaction by inviting your child to ask you questions about the story.
- Model valuable learning habits by checking information together in a book or on the internet when your child asks a question you cannot answer.
- Help your child get a library card and go to the library together to browse and check out selected books. Help children locate nonfiction books about their interests.
- Support the value of written communication by helping your child write thank-you notes, letters, and birthday cards.
- Play word games and memory games as you travel together in the car.
- Play store with items from the kitchen and real coins.
- Tape large sheets of paper to the refrigerator as a place for your child to sketch and develop drawings.
- Consider giving books and learning games as presents. What we give as presents says a lot about what we value as a family.
- Take neighborhood walks and discuss what is seen and heard.
- Enjoy music, plays, and art together and discuss the experience.

Please send a note with other ideas that work well in your family. We can collect them and share with each other in another letter.

Sincerely,

Figure 6.15 Understanding and Supporting Learning Standards

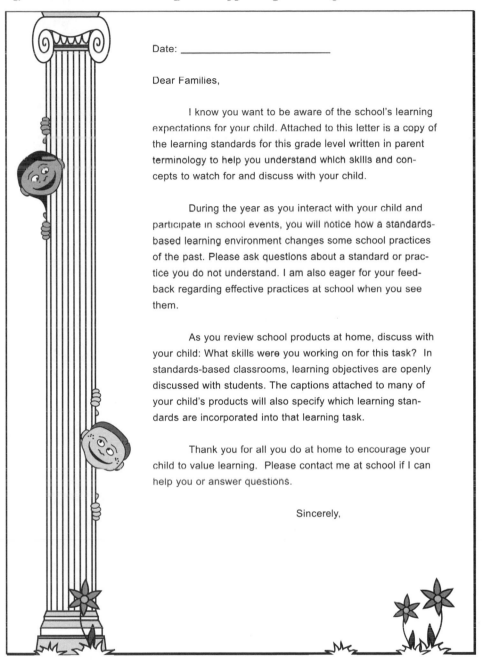

Date: _____

Dear Families,

I know you want to be aware of the school's learning expectations for your child. Attached to this letter is a copy of the learning standards for this grade level written in parent terminology to help you understand which skills and concepts to watch for and discuss with your child.

During the year as you interact with your child and participate in school events, you will notice how a standards-based learning environment changes some school practices of the past. Please ask questions about a standard or practice you do not understand. I am also eager for your feedback regarding effective practices at school when you see them.

As you review school products at home, discuss with your child: What skills were you working on for this task? In standards-based classrooms, learning objectives are openly discussed with students. The captions attached to many of your child's products will also specify which learning standards are incorporated into that learning task.

Thank you for all you do at home to encourage your child to value learning. Please contact me at school if I can help you or answer questions.

Sincerely,

7

End of the Year

T he end of the school year is a natural closure to the children's learning and assessment procedures, and it invites decisions regarding the effectiveness of the processes and the best use of collected data and documents. Educators wonder what to do with portfolios at the end of the year to insure the usefulness of the products without the information seeming overwhelming and the storage unwieldy. Hence teachers conclude the year by reflecting about the effectiveness of the assessment process, selecting products to guide the next teacher, and publishing the remaining products into individual children's books for each child to take home as a keepsake.

REFLECTION OF THE ASSESSMENT PROCESS

Effective teachers self-assess and reflect upon their instructional decisions to guide future decisions. Since the end of the year is an authentic time to review evaluation and assessment procedures, consider which of the following possibilities would be useful to refine the assessment process for next year.

Reflect Upon the Effectiveness of the Assessment System

Which components and techniques yield the most useful information and most complete view of the capacities and potentials of the children? Which processes are most productive?

Discuss With Colleagues the Value of the Assessment and Evaluation Information Shared With the Next Teacher

What is the value of this assessment and evaluation data? Would additional or different products better convey the assessment information needed to document standards and achievement levels while clarifying students' needs for future instruction?

Incorporate the PMI Strategy

The PMI strategy is an effective processing tool for reflection (DeBono, 1993). PMI stands for *plus, minus,* and *interesting.* Each word is used to guide reflection by asking participants to provide one or more responses in each category. The strategy is useful when parents respond to a menu of assessment techniques, but it is a particularly effective choice for a team of educators to use at the end of the year to prompt critical thinking and review their implementation of portfolios and other assessment procedures.

Some predictable responses include *plus* factors such as the value of the concrete data to use as evidence of students' learning growth and needs when communicating with children, parents, and educators. Other typical responses include *minus* factors concerning the time required to accomplish every goal and *interesting* factors such as how much children can do when the opportunity is well organized.

When the *plus* and *interesting* factors outweigh the *minus,* the process is clearly worthwhile. The *minus* factors identify concerns to brainstorm and problem solve as a team. As an example, a group of kindergarten and first grade teachers used the PMI strategy (Example 7.1) to critique their first year using portfolios; then they used the *minus* factors to plan improvements and set goals for the next year.

Example 7.1   Implementing Portfolios—PMI Example

Plus	Minus	Interesting
The portfolios are very useful in parent conferences.	Portfolios are new to me and seem daunting.	I love seeing the pride and success children demonstrate.
I love seeing how each child's work changes and develops.	I worry if I am doing the right thing.	Most children could do much more than I anticipated.
Portfolios offer a unique, authentic view of the child.	Scribing dictations with my four-year-olds can be very time consuming.	Portfolios make me reflect upon my teaching. The kinds of learning experiences I provided make the portfolios individual and interesting or confine the children.
Portfolios document developments the child's learning and process that cannot be recorded through standardized testing.	I manage the portfolios because I want them to be done right, but it takes too much time after school.	
	Many people still do not appreciate the amount of effort that can be put into portfolios.	

Revise the Procedures

What works efficiently and effectively and what does not? Are there easier or more efficient ways to proceed? Is there a better way to involve the children more authentically?

Elicit Parents' Feedback Regarding Which Components Provide Them With the Most Helpful Information

Create a short menu of the assessment features with which they are most directly involved such as the learning logs, letters, portfolios, and conferences with the teacher or their child. Ask the parents to rate each assessment component on a simple scale of one to five, reflecting how important or valuable each feature is to them and whether they recommend continuation of that practice with future classes.

In a Class Discussion, Elicit the Children's Perceptions of the Effectiveness of the Class Portfolio System

As much as appropriate, discuss with children what they think is working well and what needs to be changed. As young children look through their portfolios, elicit their opinions regarding their favorite products or projects to continue with next year's class. Some children may even offer ideas regarding why certain products are not effective learning experiences.

**Plan Steps to Continue Developing
Effective Assessments**

Which components can be incorporated or expanded so the process continues to result in valued information?

PRODUCTS TO GUIDE THE NEXT TEACHER

Products from the child's portfolio and anecdotes from the teacher's anecdotal folder provide valued product and process information for the next teacher. At the end of the year, initiate efficient ways to share this information about each child's achievement levels and needs to guide next year's teacher. This information enables instruction to build upon a long-term view of the development and learning needs of each student. The intent is that the next teacher is able to review concrete product and process examples in the portfolio instead of only the numbers, letters, grades, and percentages typically in school files.

One dilemma is how to share portfolio products with the next teacher while avoiding massive storage problems. Each child's entire portfolio could be sent to the next teacher so each portfolio continues for several years. This option can be exciting, but the portfolios become large and more difficult to manage. The recommended solution is for the current teacher to select a representative sample from each portfolio to pass on to the next teacher to help guide instructional planning while sending the remaining portfolio items home as a published portfolio book. With this option, the teacher selects four to ten representative items that document the child's significant accomplishments and current levels of achievement while conveying changes in learning from the beginning to the end of the year. The objective is for teachers to add to this sample each year and create a school career portfolio for each child that documents long-term achievements and learning growth. Ultimately, it can be bound and presented to the student after several years or at graduation

Teachers assume the primary responsibility for selecting products for the school career portfolio to ensure that the selected items provide the most significant information and are most representative of the child. In addition, however, mature primary children can be involved with the responsibility of selecting their best piece and writing a brief reflection to explain their thinking about their learning accomplishments. The criteria in Figure 7.1 are suggestions to focus content decisions for this ongoing record.

Figure 7.1 Products in the School Career Portfolio

Change as a learner
The teacher selects one piece from the beginning, middle, and end of the year. These pieces are chosen to document learning growth, development, and achievement by comparing work across time.

Standards, concepts, and skills
Selected products can document targeted concepts and demonstrate the transfer and application of skills.

Talents and needs
Select additional pieces as needed to substantiate special talents or needs.

Best piece
Include one product that represents the best work or highest achievement the child accomplished during the school year.

Inasmuch as both process and product are important when helping others understand a child's responses to learning opportunities, a thoughtful, succinct selection of anecdotes from the teacher's anecdotal folder is an efficient way to share observations of the child's learning processes. Attach a selection of the sticky-note anecdotes to the inside of the child's school career portfolio for easy access by the next teacher.

PUBLISHING THE YEARLY PORTFOLIO BOOKS

After selecting items for the school career portfolio, initiate the process of publishing the remaining contents into a book to be taken home as a keepsake for the child and family. If possible, plan to laminate the front and back covers of the books to protect them for years to come. The entire book could be laminated, but that process adds expense and extensive preparation time that may not result in longer lasting books.

There are several differences in the publishing process for prekindergarten and kindergarten compared to the specific process for first through third grades. Publishing the books for each group is discussed separately.

Completing Prekindergarten and Kindergarten Books

Young children's completed portfolios typically are thin and contain fewer products because much of their learning is process oriented and it may not result in a concrete product. Teachers report, however, that students are proud of these special collections and that both parents and children are thrilled to get the published books as an organized record of the year. The publishing, in addition to being an authentic closure experience, makes children's work look as important as it is.

The following is a list of typical components in young children's published portfolio books (Kingore, 2007). The teacher structures this process, but it involves the children whenever possible. Select from these suggestions and customize the process with additional features to produce books that reflect the priorities of the unique classroom environment and learning experiences. Solicit the aid of one or more parent volunteers to complete the publishing process, or organize a parent committee to assemble and bind the books.

Book Cover

Plan a front and back cover that customize each book for each child. While many different choices are possible, here are three suggestions to prompt ideas:

1. Use pictures the child draws at the beginning and the end of the year for the front and back covers. For example, the front cover can be a picture of the student or the student's family drawn at the beginning of year and dated; the back cover can be a picture of the same subject drawn at the end of year and dated.

2. Create a small collage of photographs of the child in class scenes from the beginning of the year and then the end of the year to produce visually appealing front and back covers.

3. Duplicate Figures 7.2 and 7.3 as graphic organizers that children can write on and illustrate to create the front and back covers of their portfolios. Children can add a thumbprint to the page by coloring the surface of their thumb with a water-based marker and then printing it on the page. A thumbprint is a unique feature because children know from science discussions or television that everyone's fingerprint is different.

Contents

Type and duplicate a class contents page so each child has a copy to include in the front of the portfolio before it is bound. This page is a list of the items in the book and the topics or units studied by the class. The list is organized chronologically by the dates on which each topic was completed. The order communicates to parents the sequence of the curriculum so they can understand how specific products relate to learning objectives and more appropriately gauge the progression of the child's skill growth and development.

Poem. Consider including a poem that addresses the philosophy of your class such as Dorothy Law Nolte's *Children Learn What They Live* (Nolte, 2001; Nolte & Harris, 1998). Parents benefit from these gentle reminders of developmentally appropriate practices and expectations for young children.

Figure 7.2 Portfolio Front Cover

About the author. The about the author form (Figure 7.4) helps personalize each portfolio book with the child's photograph and list of favorite things. The children writing in their temporary (invented) spelling or the older students, aides, or parent volunteers acting as scribes who record the children's dictations can complete the sentence stems. When appropriate, challenge children to design a pattern to decorate the border of the page.

Figure 7.3 Portfolio Back Cover

Products. The products the teacher and the child select throughout the year are the main feature of the portfolio. These products are dated, organized in chronological order, and included to illustrate the child's learning changes and skill growth during the year.

Friends and classmates. Young learners enjoy the experience of collecting autographs from classmates. Include one or two pages titled *Friends and Classmates* as a place where children in the class can write their names or draw small pictures in each other's books after the portfolios are bound.

Figure 7.4 About the Author

About the Author

I like to play _____

I like to eat _____

At home, I like _____

I want to be a _____

My favorite thing at school is _____

My favorite book is _____

I wish _____

My photograph

Binding

Complete the publishing process by binding each portfolio book. Plastic comb bindings produce an attractive finished product and are available at copy shops if not at the school. Additional simple binding procedures include three-hole punching to organize pages in a notebook or hole-punched pages using metal rings, yarn, or ribbon to hold the book together.

Completing First- Through Third-Grade Books

Compared to the portfolios of the prekindergarten and kindergarten children, the portfolios of primary children contain a wider sample of work that often includes one product selected every one or two weeks of school. Parents and children love having these books as an organized record of learning experiences and growth throughout the year.

Connecting Learning Experience

Learning About the Parts of Books

To initiate the publishing process with first-, second-, and third-grade children, encourage them to look through library books and analyze the parts of these published works. Together, compose a list of the parts of books that they identify, and then plan together how to incorporate as many of those features into their portfolio books as appropriate. The intent is for children to feel that published portfolios are as important as a commercially published book.

The teacher organizes this publishing process and completes it collaboratively with the children. The children's active involvement is a crucial catalyst to their pride in the finished products. The following is a list of potential components typical in primary children's published portfolio books (Kingore, 2007). Select from these suggestions and customize with any additional features from the class-generated list to produce books that reflect the children's preferences, the priorities of your classroom-learning environment, and the learning experiences that are representative of your curriculum.

Book Cover

Select any of the book cover suggestions discussed for the prekindergarten and kindergarten children or encourage primary children to design their own book covers by inviting them to use their favorite colors and personalize this special book with illustrations of their interests and/or favorite things. The covers are particularly effective when children design and date the front cover at the beginning of the year and complete the back cover and date it at the end of the year.

Title Page

After brainstorming and recording examples on the board, primary children can write and decorate a title page complete with an inventive publishing company that incorporates the school's name, the copyright year for their book, and the teacher's name as the editor. Title examples include *My Treasury from Mrs. Wilhelm's Second-Grade Class* and *My First-Grade Learning Adventures.*

Dedication Page

Children can create a dedication page to include in their portfolio books. It is interesting to see to whom students dedicate their books. Frequently, young children dedicate their books to a family member and further validate the important influence of the home environment on learning aspirations. Sometimes, they dedicate their book to their teacher because they love their teacher. This dedication is a wonderful validation of the caring and often difficult work a teacher demonstrates when helping students succeed and learn.

Contents

A contents page helps organize the book and has additional application value when the children are actively involved. Teachers report that after children create a contents page for their portfolio, they begin to use the table of contents in other books with renewed interest and ability.

Figure 7.5 is a template for a contents page with at least two application possibilities. The teacher can complete the page by writing the month and listing topics or general categories of included products each month before duplicating a copy for each child's portfolio. However, as an alternative that involves an authentic writing task, the teacher duplicates the pages after listing only the months in chronological order. Then children use that duplicated outline to record the title of each item they include in their portfolio for each month. Finally, children personalize the page by illustrating the border space surrounding the contents.

Portfolio ticket. A portfolio ticket delineates the categories and sequence of child selected items that the teacher determines should be placed in the published portfolio book. This technique enables children with beginning writing and organization skills to be more involved in the publishing process by providing a concrete guide for children as they organize their products into a portfolio book. The teacher lists the category menu; children follow the menu to select their product examples for each category. Each listed item is numbered and has a simple geometric shape with a color word beside it. The teacher duplicates the ticket so each child has a copy. Children color each shape as they place the listed product in their portfolio in the sequence listed on the ticket. They add a corresponding colored shape on the top right-hand corner of each selected product so others understand which item that product represents. Figure 7.6 is a template for a portfolio ticket.

Figure 7.5 Contents Template

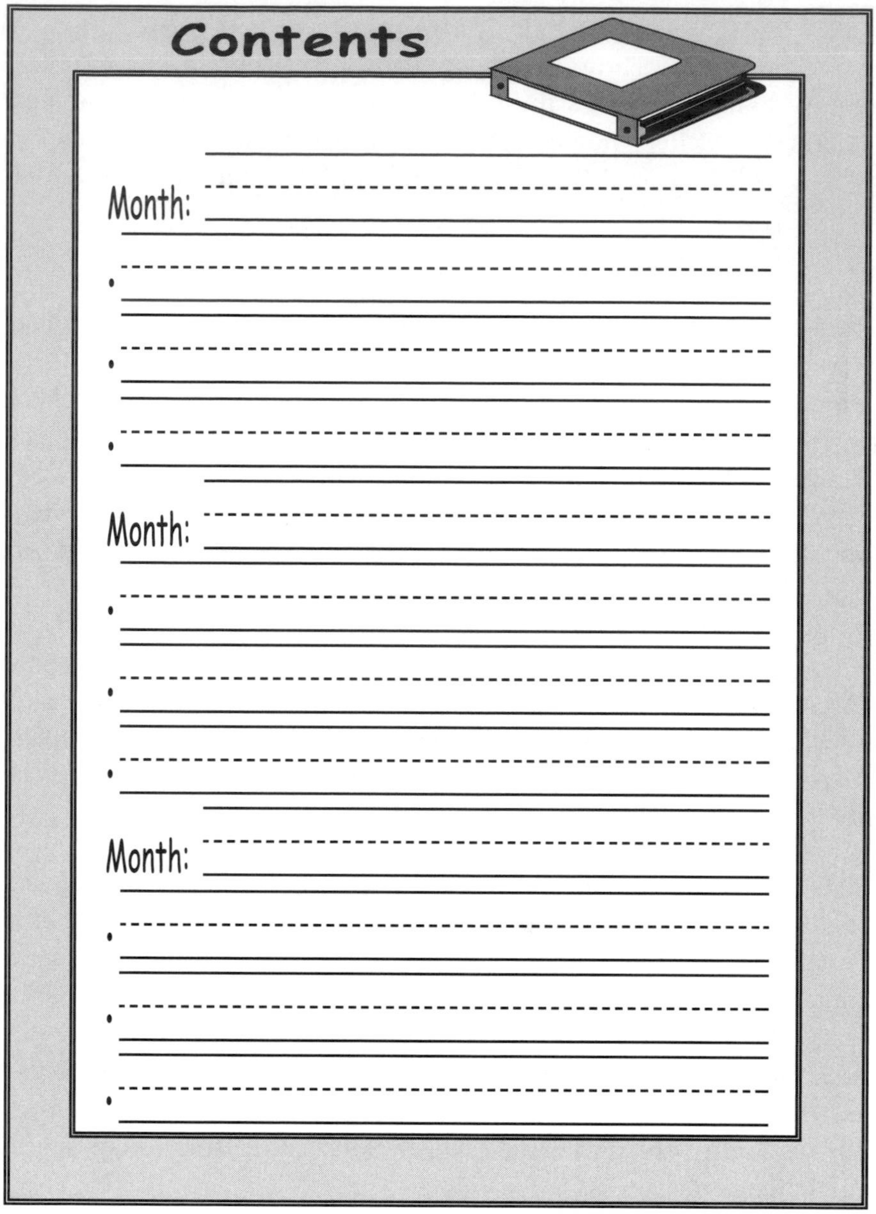

Contents

Month: _____

• _____

• _____

• _____

Month: _____

• _____

• _____

• _____

Month: _____

• _____

• _____

• _____

Autobiography. To simulate the author information that is often included on the book jacket of a published book, each child writes a paragraph or more about themselves as the author. Including a photograph from home or school on the front or back of the page adds visual interest and highlights the child. As an alternative, some children may prefer to draw their portrait.

Brainstorm with the class the kinds of information and a bank of words they might use to write about themselves in their autobiography. Encourage analytical thinking by asking them to explain as they elaborate their responses. As an alternative, provide copies of Figure 7.7 if children would benefit from more structure to guide their writing. Invite children to use the border space on that template to personalize the page by illustrating small pictures of things about their life and things they like.

Figure 7.6 Portfolio Ticket

Figure 7.7 Autobiography

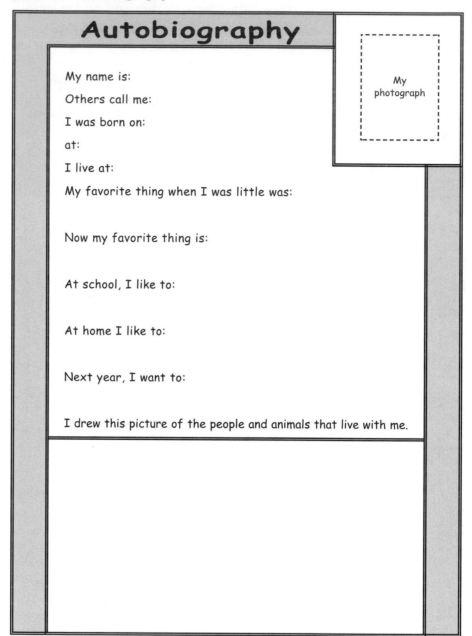

Autobiography

My name is:

Others call me:

I was born on:

at:

I live at:

My favorite thing when I was little was:

Now my favorite thing is:

At school, I like to:

At home I like to:

Next year, I want to:

I drew this picture of the people and animals that live with me.

My photograph

Connecting Learning Experience

Children's Dictation

At the beginning of the year, use copies of the about the author page with small groups of students as a teacher-directed language arts activity. While the teacher interacts with one child at a time and records on the front or back of the form the embellished responses dictated by the child, the other children in the small group are encouraged to write, draw pictures, and design a patterned border to personalize the front of their page (Figure 7.4).

This task is an assessment that provides information about many aspects of children's readiness, such as oral language development, fine motor coordination, patterns, and emergent literacy skills. At the end of the year, this beginning form is compared with the child's autobiography. These two products are an interesting way to elicit children's changing views of their abilities and preferences.

Products and captions. The main feature of a portfolio book is the products systematically selected during the year by the teacher and children. Dated and organized in chronological sequence, the products document the child's learning changes and skill growth throughout the year. The captions on each product reveal the children's attitudes and perceptions about their learning.

Highlights of the year. Highlights of the year is a memory page about the events during the school year that children most enjoyed or want to remember. The content for the page can be developed as a class project near the end of the school year by brainstorming and listing on a chart the events that children recall. Later, on a copy of a highlights page, each child records the special events he or she wants to include and why each event is a highlight. It is fascinating to read children's selections.

Friends and classmates. As with the prekindergarten and kindergarten books, include one or two pages titled *Friends and Classmates.* As a closure task after the portfolios are bound, classes conduct portfolio book signings during which classmates write graffiti-style messages to one another.

Reflections. Place a blank page at the end of the portfolio book entitled *Reflections* as a space where people can add notes over time. Discuss with the children and share with their parents that, when they revisit this book, they can record the date and write a note about how they now feel about the contents.

Binding

Complete the publication process by binding the portfolio books in some way such as using any of the suggestions shared for binding the prekindergarten and kindergarten books. Arrange for a parent volunteer, aide, or older students to assist in completing the process of binding the portfolios. When several classes in the building are publishing portfolios, collectively communicate needs and coordinate the use of materials and equipment so that not everyone attempts to complete the process at the same time.

CELEBRATING THE PUBLISHED PORTFOLIO BOOKS

Portfolios involve a yearlong process and are a significant component in the children's learning environment. The published portfolio books enable children to experience high self-esteem by recognizing children's efforts and progress instead of just their achievements. Often, children voice great pride in their work as they look back at what they have accomplished. As one excited four-year-old exclaimed to her friend at the end of the year, "I know a lot!" Then she turned to a page in her portfolio book from the beginning of the year and explained, "Look at this baby stuff. I did this when I was little." Highlight the significance of these published books by arranging a class celebration as a scheduled time to share the books before they are taken home.

Connecting Learning Experience

Preparing Refreshments With Individual Recipes

The class can work together to prepare refreshments for the portfolio book celebration. Incorporate math and literacy skills with a cooking activity in which the children follow recipes or sequence charts to make refreshments as part of the preparation for the celebration. Rather than use a group recipe where an adult does most of the preparation while the children watch, adapt simple recipes to individual portions so each child is actively involved in producing the treats. For example, if the recipe calls for two cups of flour (which is thirty-two tablespoons) and there are twenty-four children, each child uses one tablespoon plus one teaspoon of flour to make an individual portion.

Noncooking recipes such as sugar-free powder drinks and no-bake cookies are appealing alternatives when cooking equipment is limited. This learning experience is also an authentic time to model and require healthy habits such as washing hands frequently.

1. As the children receive their published portfolio books for the first time, use chart paper and record their comments and reactions as a language experience. Their responses document the pleasure and pride the portfolio books evoke from each author. Consider incorporating some of their reactions in a letter to the parents.

2. Continue the celebration by providing an opportunity for children to share the published portfolios. Pair the children and let them read their books to each other.

3. Complete the celebration with an opportunity for children to autograph one another's books before taking them home.

4. Arrange to videotape the children as they share and talk about their published books during the celebration. It will be a great motivator when introducing the portfolio process to next year's class.

5. Before sending the books home, write a letter to send to the families announcing when the portfolio books will arrive. Help home members appreciate how important these books are to each child, as the contents represent significant learning accomplishments throughout the entire year. A sample letter is included in Figure 7.8. Personalize the letter by inviting children to write their names in the blank: A Very Special Announcement About _____. Children can draw a picture at the bottom of the page or the teacher can use that space to include several of the comments children made when they received their published portfolio books for the first time.

Figure 7.8 Family Letter: Portfolio Books

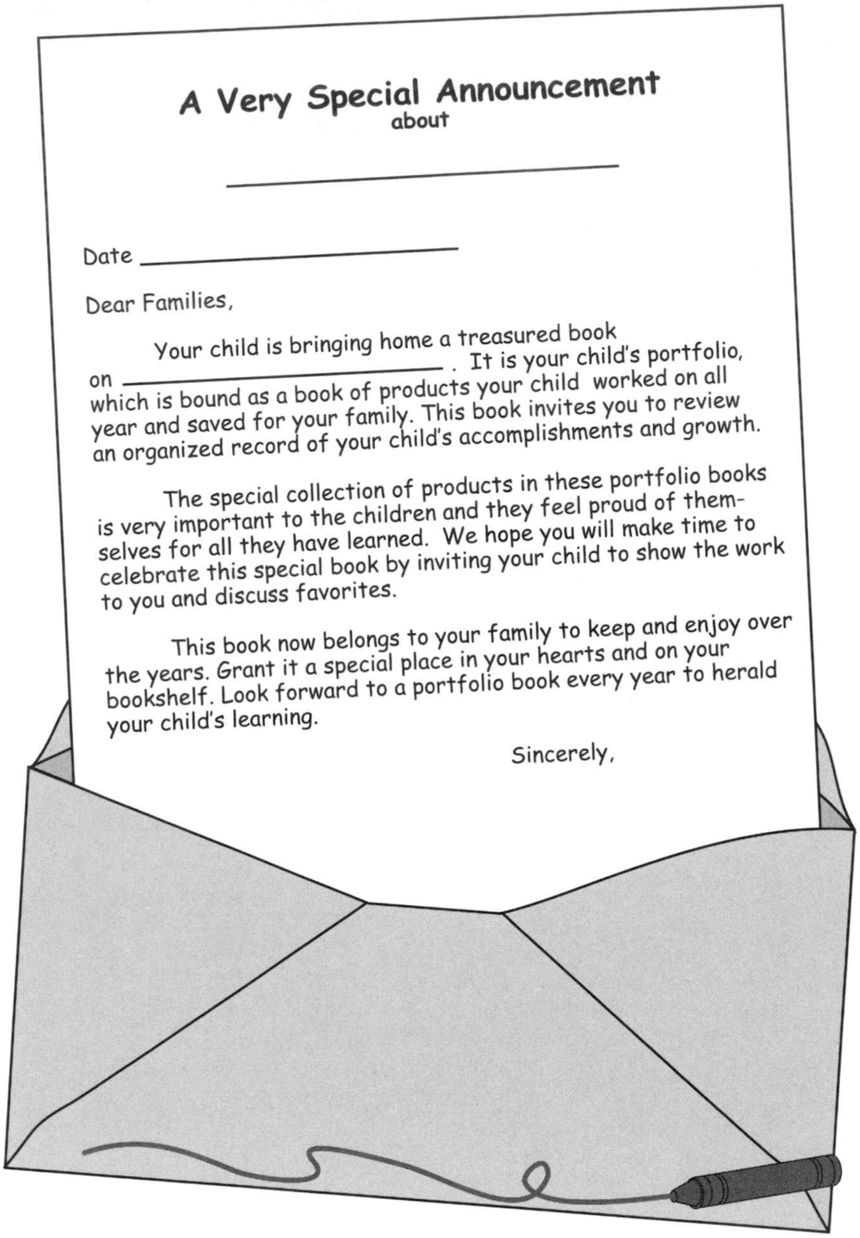

A Very Special Announcement
about

_____

Date _____

Dear Families,

Your child is bringing home a treasured book
on _____ . It is your child's portfolio,
which is bound as a book of products your child worked on all
year and saved for your family. This book invites you to review
an organized record of your child's accomplishments and growth.

The special collection of products in these portfolio books
is very important to the children and they feel proud of themselves for all they have learned. We hope you will make time to
celebrate this special book by inviting your child to show the work
to you and discuss favorites.

This book now belongs to your family to keep and enjoy over
the years. Grant it a special place in your hearts and on your
bookshelf. Look forward to a portfolio book every year to herald
your child's learning.

Sincerely,

Appendix: Stationery Templates

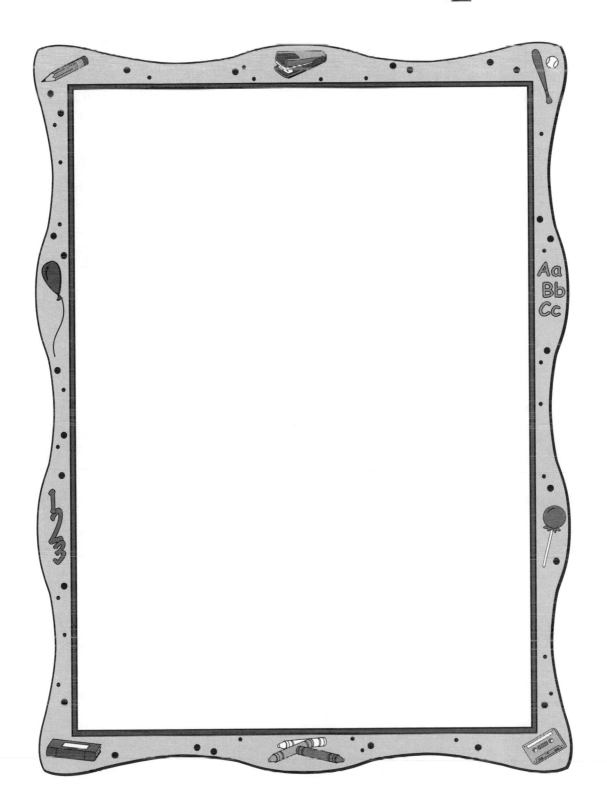

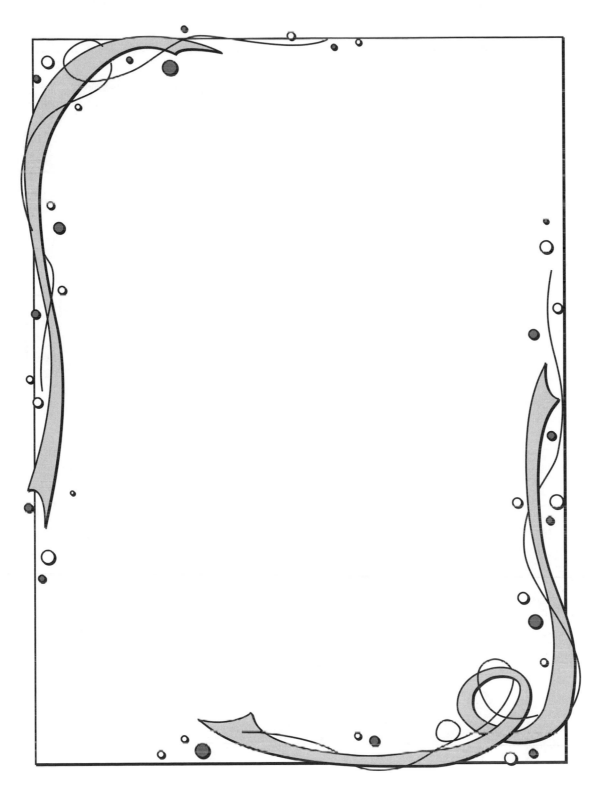

References

Anderson, L., & Krathwohl, D. (Eds.). (2001). *A taxonomy for learning, teaching, and assessing: A revision of Bloom's taxonomy of educational objectives.* New York: Addison-Wesley Longman.

Association for Supervision and Curriculum Development. (2006a). *Multiple measures of assessment: Policy paper.* Alexandria, VA: Author.

Association for Supervision and Curriculum Development. (2006b). *Building academic vocabulary: Research-based, comprehensive strategies. Research Report.* Alexandria, VA: Author.

Bergen, D. (2002). The role of pretend play in children's cognitive development. *Early Childhood Research and Practice, 4*(1). Retrieved January 7, 2007, from http://ecrp.uiuc.edu/v4n1/bergen.html

Berk, L., & Winsler, Z. (1995). *Scaffolding children's learning: Vygotsky and early childhood education.* Washington, DC: National Association for the Education of Young Children.

Black, P., & William, D. (1998, October). Inside the black box: Raising standards through classroom assessment. *Phi Delta Kappan,* 139–149.

Burke, K. (2005). *How to assess authentic learning* (4th ed.). Thousand Oaks, CA: Corwin Press.

Caine, R., Caine, G., Klimek, K., & McClintic, C. (2004). *12 Brain/mind learning principles in action.* Thousand Oaks, CA: SAGE.

Collins, M., & Amabile, T. (1999). Motivation and creativity. In R. Sternberg (Ed.), *Handbook of creativity* (pp. 297–312). Cambridge, MA: Cambridge University Press.

Commission on the Whole Child. (2007). *The whole child.* Alexandria, VA: Association for Supervision and Curriculum Development.

De Bono, E. (1993). *Teach your child how to think.* New York: Penguin Books.

Eisner, E. (2005). Back to whole. *Educational Leadership, 63*(1), 14–18.

Erickson, H. (2007). *Concept-based curriculum and instruction for the thinking classroom.* Thousand Oaks, CA: Corwin Press

Gardner, H. (1996, Spring). Your child's intelligence(s). *Scholastic Parent & Child,* 32–37.

Grigorenko, E., & Sternberg, R. (1997). Styles of thinking, abilities, and academic performance. *Exceptional Children, 63,* 295–312.

Herman, J., Baker, E., & Linn, R. (2004). Accountability systems in support of student learning: Moving to the next generation. *CRESST LINE*. Los Angeles: University of California, National Center for Research on Evaluation, Standards, and Student Testing.

Hertzog, N. (1998). Open-ended activities: Differentiation through learner responses. *Gifted Child Quarterly, 42,* 212–227.

High/Scope Educational Research Foundation. (2005). *Lifetime effects: The High/Scope Perry preschool study through age 40.* Ypsilanti, MI: Author.

Jones, J. (2003). *Early literacy assessment systems: Essential elements.* Princeton, NJ: Educational Testing Service.

Karoly, L. (2005). *Early childhood interventions: Proven results, future promise.* Santa Monica, CA: RAND.

Kingore, B. (2001). *Kingore observation inventory (KOI)* (2nd ed.). Austin, TX: Professional Associates Publishing.

Kingore, B. (2007). *Assessment: Time-saving procedures for busy teachers* (4th ed.). Austin, TX: Professional Associates Publishing.

Levy, A., Wolfgang, C., & Koorland, M. (1992). Sociodramatic play as a method for enhancing the language performance of kindergarten age students. *Early Childhood Research Quarterly, 7*(2), 245–262.

MacDonald, S. (2005). *The portfolio and its use: A roadmap for assessment* (2nd ed.). Little Rock, AR: Southern Early Childhood Association.

Marcon, R. (2002). Moving up the grades: Relationship between preschool model and later school success. *Early Childhood Research and Practice, 4*(1). Retrieved January 12, 2007, from http://ecrp.uiuc.edu/v4n1/marcon.html

Marzano, R. (2004). *Building background knowledge for academic achievement: Research on what works in schools.* Alexandria, VA: Association for Supervision and Curriculum Development.

Marzano, R., Pickering, D., & Pollock, J. (2001). *Classroom instruction that works: Research-based strategies for increasing student achievement.* Alexandria, VA: Association for Supervision and Curriculum Development.

National Association for the Education of Young Children. (1997). *Developmentally appropriate practice in early childhood programs serving children from birth through age 8. Position statement.* Washington, DC: Author.

National Association for the Education of Young Children & National Association of Early Childhood Specialists in State Departments of Education. (2003). *Early childhood curriculum, assessment, and program evaluation: Building an effective, accountable system in programs for children birth through age 8. Position statement.* Washington, DC: Author.

National Association of Elementary School Principals & Collaborative Communications Group. (2005). *Leading early childhood learning communities: What principals should know and be able to do.* Alexandria, VA: Author.

National Council of Teachers of Mathematics & National Association for the Education of Young Children. (2002). *Early childhood mathematics: Promoting good beginnings. Position statement.* Washington, DC: Author.

National Reading Panel. (2000). *Teaching children to read: An evidence-based assessment of the scientific research literature on reading and its implications for reading instruction.* Jessup, MD: National Institute for Literacy.

Nelson, A. (2006). Closing the gap: Early childhood education. *ASCD Infobrief, 45*, 1–9.

Noddings, N. (2005). What does it mean to educate the whole child? *Educational Leadership, 63*(1), 8–13.

Nolte, D. (2001). Children learn what they live. In J. Canfield & M. Hansen (Eds.), *Chicken soup for the soul* (pp. 85–86). Deerfield Beach, FL: Health Communications.

Nolte, D., & Harris, R. (1998). *Children learn what they live: Parenting to inspire values.* New York: Workman Publishing.

Payne, R. (2003). *A framework for understanding poverty* (3rd ed.) Highlands, TX: aha! Process, Inc.

Potter, E. (1999). What should I put in my portfolio? Supporting young children's goals and evaluations. *Childhood Education, 75*, 210–214.

Ratcliff, N. (2001). Using authentic assessment to document the emerging literacy skills of young children. *Childhood Education, 78*, 66–68.

Rothstein, R. (2006). The social and economic realities that challenge all schools: Independent, charter, and regular public schools alike. *Independent School, 65*(2), 18–26.

Scott-Little, C., Kagan, S., & Frelow, V. (2003). Creating the conditions for success with early learning standards: Results from a national study of state-level standards for children's learning prior to kindergarten. *Early Childhood Research and Practice, 5*, 2. Retrieved February 28, 2007, from http://ecrp.uiuc.edu/v5n2/index.html

Shepard, L. (1997). *Measuring achievement: What does it mean to test for robust understanding?* Princeton, NJ: Educational Testing Service.

Shepard, L., Kagan, S., & Wirtz, E. (1998). *Principles and recommendations for early childhood assessment.* Washington, DC: National Education Goals Panel.

Smutny, J., Walker, S., & Meckstroth, E. (2007). *Acceleration for gifted learners, K–5.* Thousand, Oaks, CA: Corwin Press.

Sousa, D. (2001). *How the brain learns* (2nd ed.). Thousand Oaks, CA: Corwin Press.

Stiggins, R. (2005). *Using student-involved classroom assessment to close achievement gaps* (4th ed.). Columbus, OH: Merrill Prentice Hall.

Stronge, J. (2002). *Qualities of effective teachers.* Alexandria, VA: Association for Supervision and Curriculum Development.

Sylwester, R. (2003). *A biological brain in a cultural classroom* (2nd ed.). Thousand Oaks, CA: Corwin Press.

Tomlinson, C. (2003). *Fulfilling the promise of the differentiated classroom.* Alexandria, VA: Association for Supervision and Curriculum Development.

Vygotsky, L. (1962). *Thought and language.* Cambridge, MA: MIT Press.

Wiggins, G., & McTighe, J. (2005). *Understanding by design* (2nd ed.). Alexandria, VA: Association for Supervision and Curriculum Development.

Willis, J. (2006). *Research-based strategies to ignite student learning: Insights from a neurologist and classroom teacher.* Alexandria, VA: Association for Supervision and Curriculum Development.

Woodward, H. (2000). Portfolios: Narratives for learning. *Journal of In-Service Education, 26*(2), 329–349.

Young, E. (1992). *Seven blind mice.* New York: Scholastic.

Index